SURVIV
TO
CRUISING

Survival Guide
To
Cruising

Vaughan Robinson

BLOOTOAD

Publisher's Note

The following book is for enrichment purposes only, and the author and publisher can take no responsibility for how this information is used or acted upon.

First published in Great Britain & America in 2019 by Blootoad

First published in paperback in 2019

A CIP catalogue record of this title is available from the British Library

ISBN

978-0-9570738-2-1

Typeset in Garamond

Printed and bound by Create Space Print on Demand

Blootoad

Note:

The following book is for enrichment purposes only, and the author and publisher can take no responsibility for how this information is used or acted upon.

Contents

To my lovely mum, who has always encouraged me to write

Introduction

With cruising being the vacation of choice for many in recent years, you could perhaps be forgiven for thinking that it is a relatively new concept, but cruising in one form or another been around for longer than you might imagine.

In the mid 19th century innovation was coming from the industrial revolution, steam was replacing sail, and modern construction techniques using steel instead of wood meant that ships could be made to a much grander scale. This change had an almost immediate impact upon the volume and the type of goods being shipped around the world.

By the end of the 19th century, companies such as the White Star Line were building large ocean going ships to cater for an increasingly growing cargo travelling the Atlantic - passengers. Unlike other cargo, however, most passengers wanted a little more comfort than a dank, dark, confined hole, full of rats and coal, although those travelling steerage-class (second/third-class) might have questioned their perceived comfort to that of a rat.

For those passengers prepared to part with ludicrous amounts of money, a journey of opulence and luxury could be expected when they stepped aboard a transatlantic passenger ship. Grand staircases designed with a distinct regal feel swept majestically from floor to floor. Artisan designed interiors were adorned with art from old masters and the upcoming avant-garde artists. As in fashionable seaside resorts one could promenade in refined clothing along the extensive decks, or mingle with other passengers in the many restaurants and cocktail bars aboard. In a further desire to keep 'discerning' passengers entertained, cruise ships also had swimming pools, Turkish baths, tennis courts, theatres, ball rooms, and plush dining areas.

Going into the 20th century ocean travel was becoming so popular with people, more shipping companies became involved offering ever more places to explore. It was the time when the ocean going ship not only took passengers to destinations, the ship had become a destination in its own right, and cruising as we understand it today was born.

There are surprisingly many similarities between cruising then and now, and a quick glance at any cruise brochure or internet site will highlight the luxuries you can expect aboard the modern cruise ship. There is, however, one main difference between then and now – cruising in comfort has become much more affordable in recent years. You need not have won the lottery, have been bequeathed a fortune by a great aunt, or sold your soul to the devil to afford a cruise – far from it. Even if you are on a tight budget it is still possible to take a cruise and have access to all the luxuries and service so synonymous with this form of travel. For a surprisingly small outlay you can emulate those wealthy cruise passengers of yesteryear and promenade decks, sip cocktails, relax in the ships Spa, and be pampered to your hearts content.

With that said, don't be lulled into a false sense of security and believe you won't finish the cruise having spent much more than you originally anticipated. Even with the affordability of luxury cruising opening up too many more, you may find yourself haemorrhaging money at an alarming rate if you aren't careful. You may even discover that the luxury you were expecting aboard leaves a lot to be desired when you are confronted with a small, dark space, sandwiched in-between the engine room and the crew bar when you are shown into your cabin.

But don't worry, help is here at hand!

It is with these issues in mind and many more for that matter, Survival Guide to Cruising has been written. Having a vacation that fulfils your expectations in regards to comfort, price, and a host of other equally important requirements is paramount for all I am sure. This guidebook is designed to make you aware of the many aspects you may come across that might have a negative impact on your cruise, and it specifically highlights ways to avoid them.

My Credentials

I have spent over 4 years on cruise ships as a crewmember, but unlike many of my colleagues, my position aboard in guest services gave me passenger privileges. Over the years these special privileges have afforded me the opportunity to go on over 1000 tours, attend hundreds of onboard shows, have countless spa treatments, and dine in many onboard restaurants. I have also been able to explore the majority of places cruise ships frequent around the world, including having taken world cruises, and many multiple day overland excursions. As a crewmember I was able to dig out little nuggets of information from each department that would help to assist cruise passengers. This gave me a breadth of understanding that would have been more difficult to attain as a passenger. (A fuller explanation of my position aboard cruise ships can be found in another book entitled, Robinson Cruising.) Whilst I can't profess to have all the answers, I do try to address aspects of cruising that I believe will be pertinent to many people taking a cruise.

Those New to Cruising

If you are new to cruising, take some time to look at the table of contents, and get a feel for the type of subjects discussed. Whilst you can certainly read the guidebook in its entirety from start to finish, some chapters will be more relevant than others at certain stages of your cruise, so don't be afraid to dip in and out of this guide when the need should arise. Each chapter is of equal length and has a section at the end entitled 'Tips', which is designed to act as a quick summery of the key points within each chapter. Whilst all of the guidebook should be relevant to you I have also included a specific section near the end of the book entitled - Top Tips for First Time Cruisers. This chapter brings together key pieces of information from the guidebook to act as a quick reference for you. At the end of the book I have also included a 'Tick List' of essential items to take on your cruise, so you don't leave something potentially important behind.

The Seasoned Cruiser

Let me be clear at the outset, reading this guidebook is not going to be a completely revelatory experience if you are a regular cruiser. Let's face it, we are talking about cruising after all said and done, I haven't just come up with a new theory on the binary ambiguities of cultural and class dimorphism. I am fully aware that some of what I say may be considered too basic or just common sense for the reasoned cruiser, or indeed anyone for that matter; but if I don't mention something because I think the reader will know it already, and they don't, I am not doing my job properly in writing a guide.

My hope is that you can add to, or perhaps tweak your knowledge of cruising. I am a firm believer that no matter what our knowledge or experience we can all learn something new, even if it means sifting through things we know already or it comes from some jumped-up crewmember.

What this guide does not do

This guide does not grade one cruise company against another, drill down into prices you should expect to pay for each cruise/activity, or include any photographs, maps, or glossy images pertinent to cruising. The format of this guidebook is specifically to inform you on what to expect with cruising in general. That is not to say it is generalised in its discussion about cruising – far from it. It has detailed information about many aspects of cruising, whilst being compact and portable for ease of transport. If you are specifically after ship layouts, maps of ports, images of specific ships, or comparisons between cruise companies, I suggest you look to websites and other well regarded cruise guide books.

Survival Guide to Cruising is full of facts and practical information presented in a compact and easily navigable form. It has been specifically designed to assist you with planning a cruise on an American, European, or indeed any other flagged cruise ship – I just hope you can embrace my humour, as it makes an appearance occasionally throughout.

1

Deals

Everyone likes to feel they are getting a deal in some way, it often makes it easier to sanction the amount of money that will be spent, and finding those deals is something many of us have become very proficient at in recent years. With many companies offering the best deals for new customers instead of rewarding loyalty, it seems almost every month we are called upon to look for a new deal in one form or another. The comparison website deals, pop-up deals, black Friday deals, early booking deals, late booking deals, referral deals, birthday deals, and even dastardly dodgy deals are negotiated by us on a regular basis. For this reason, I appreciate it would be churlish of me to sport with your intelligence and talk you piecemeal on how to find a great deal, so I am only going to point out a few things to be mindful of when it comes to booking cruising deals specifically.

General Deals

When booking any cruise, it is important to make sure you check exactly what you are getting in the deal, and read the description thoroughly. Don't assume that an all inclusive deal will include all food, bottled water, all alcohol, and so forth. It might be that only certain beverages and food are provided at specific venues and times of day, and you might need to upgrade your deal to get what you want. If you consistently have to tick the upgrade box whilst you are booking a cruise it might be cheaper to book a more expensive package with these upgrades included as standard. For instance, it can sometimes be cheaper to book a deluxe suit cabin than a standard cabin with add-on upgrades.

What I am saying is, read the deals being offered by cruise lines or travel agents forensically to be sure of not being disappointed when you get aboard. If you don't do this, you may well find that what you originally thought was the all inclusive deal, turns out to be the all exclusive deal.

Last Minute Deals

Whilst some last minute cruise deals can certainly save you money there are a few things to be aware of before booking them. You might see a last-minute deal on the internet and it outlines the cruise itinerary, specific ship, and what seems like a good deal. In instances like these be prepared to dig a little because the offer you see might tell you what you do get, but avoid highlighting what you don't get; or should that be, what you will get, but will have to pay more to get it, even if you didn't want it in the first place.

Ask yourself questions such as, does the deal include **taxes, port charges, handling fees, fuel surcharge, and government fees**? These can significantly increase the price you pay for a cruise if not included, and you will have to factor them into the overall price if they aren't. In addition to this, many last minute deals give you a very limited choice when it comes to the cabins that are available. This could mean you get a cabin that is not suitable, either because of its position, size, or proximity to noisy areas of the ship (choosing an appropriate cabin will be discussed in chapter 15). You might even be expected to pay for some activities, certain foods and entertainment, which may well have been included in the price of a cruise booked in advance. In addition to this, some last minute cruise deals do not include flights, and any savings made on a cruise may well be eaten-up paying for a last minute flight (assuming one is needed).

Identifying exactly what is included and what is not included in a deal is essential, but it may not be as transparent as you hoped, and you may need to contact the company advertising the cruise for additional information. If you book your cruise on the internet, make sure they have a local or cheap rate number you can contact them on before booking. Don't get stung calling high tariff numbers only to be placed on hold for so long the cost of the call could have paid for a deluxe suite cabin upgrade instead of the box room next to the ships engine, which is all you thought you could afford. That is not to say you can't ask any questions you may have over the internet, but it can sometimes be difficult to get prompt replies, and often you can't get the answers to the questions you really want.

It all sounds a bit grim doesn't it? But I am not saying that all last minute deals are trying to rip you off or offer a lesser product, I am just giving you a few things to be mindful of before booking one. In my experience people tend to gloss over certain things when they think there may be a bargain to be had last minute, and this is precisely the time that extra scrutiny should be given to a deal.

Early Booking Deals

Cruise companies don't want to encourage a culture where people wait until last minute to get a deal because the uncertainty of sales puts more pressure on advertising, which ultimately means less profit for them. To counteract this, many cruise companies are keen to encourage people to book in advance, and generally offer the best deals for those that book early. It also means you have a greater choice from the cabins onboard, and whilst you might not be able to pick a specific cabin with all cruise lines, you can at least get the category you want, whilst knowing you are getting an excellent deal.

Many cruise companies reward loyalty, and if you join loyalty programs and book another cruise with the same company you can often get a better deal. Early booking deals are also available when you are on a cruise, and most cruise companies generally have a future cruises room or a specific area on the ship for you to enquire about other cruises they have. Booking a cruise this way can mean free cabin upgrades, bonus money towards meals, smaller deposits, and credits towards tour excursions. Some cruise lines also offer price tracker deals, meaning the price you pay for your cruise will be reduced if the price goes down on a like-for-like basis. As with booking many other cruises, you can generally cancel the cruise should you wish without forfeiting your deposit, as long as this is done by a certain date (I would recommend you make a note of this date because you never know if you may need to cancel).

A word of warning – not all cruise companies have the same cancellation policies, and just because one cruise company has a refundable deposit if you cancel 30 days before a cruise, it doesn't mean another company will do the same. Added to this, when the period for a refund has passed you may be expected to pay more than just the refund should you cancel, and the amount you pay after this period goes up incrementally the closer you get to the date of the ship sailing. If you don't turn up for the cruise, you may be expected to pay for the whole thing, including taxes and so forth, even if you cancel due to illness or death in the family you may still have to pay taxes and such like. Paying on credit cards can help with recouping some of this money in some circumstances (through your cards inbuilt insurance).

One thing is for sure – seriously consider travel insurance, and make sure you read the small print on that as well, so you can be sure you are covered properly (this will be covered in more depth later in the guide). You certainly don't want to lose a substantial deposit or have to pay even more than your deposit because of not checking the small print. Reading the small print might have all the appeal of hitting your thumb consistently with a hammer for hours, but if it saves you money or stress it might be time well spent.

Tips

1. Being loyal to one cruise company means there will be more opportunities for add-ons such as cabin upgrades, cheaper cruises and such like.
2. Make sure you know what it means when it says all-inclusive cruise, and find out exactly **what is and what isn't** included in your deal.
3. Organising your own transport (plane flights, trains, and shuttles) means you may not get a refund for the cruise if your flight is delayed and you miss the ship. It is also advisable to arrive at least a day early and stay in a local hotel if you are organising your own flights to a cruise.
4. Last minute deals might be cheap, but if you have to fly to the cruise, finding a reasonably priced flight last minute can be quite difficult if not included in the deal.
5. Those passengers new to cruising might do well to take a short cruise to see if they like it.
6. When booking your cruise ask if handling fees, taxes, port charges, fuel surcharge, and government fees are included in the price.
7. Look at the cancellation policies of the cruise line you will be traveling with, and remember, illness and death of a loved one may not see you getting a refund – **read the cruise contract thoroughly, take out appropriate travel insurance, and make sure you read the small print to be sure you are covered appropriately.**

2

Choosing a Cruise

Finding cheap cruise deals should not be your sole consideration because it could mean other important aspects of cruising fall by the wayside. Subscribing to too many websites in the hunt for a cheap deal might also find your inbox so full of junk-mail it takes a virus to clear it out. With this in mind, this chapter is designed to highlight a few things you might want to consider before choosing a cruise, and making cheap deals your priority.

Types of Cruise

It has often been suggested that all cruises are for retired people with deep pockets, but this is no longer true – if indeed it was true in the first place. Cruise companies cater for all ages and budgets, although you will need to choose the company and ship that best suits your needs and requirements. This is because each cruise company tries to market and appeal to a specific demographic - families with children, activity seekers, mature couples, those wanting to explore ports, and so forth. The facilities, entertainment, activities, tours, food and even the design of the ship are often very different. For instance, the family oriented cruises very often visit fewer ports, and the ship acts as a resort were emphasis is placed upon passengers utilising the facilities aboard. These cruises can have larger youth areas and activities for different ages such as, play rooms, crèches, games rooms, discos, zip lines, big screens and so forth. Even the tours on these cruises are geared towards families, and they generally offer fewer opportunities for the culture seeker.

Conversely, if you have a family and the cruise focuses on ports, you might not have time to fully engage with the activities aboard as more time will be spent visiting ports ashore. You may also find that entertainment and facilities aboard are paired down, smaller youth areas, and reduced entertainment aboard for example. On these cruises you can forego going ashore and use the ships facilities such as swimming pools, and spa when the ship is in port, but you may find some activities and certain entertainment is not available (this is mainly due to maritime law, laws of the country you are visiting, reduced staffing, and crew drills taking place). Port focused cruises also have a tendency to increase what you spend over the cruise, especially if you are going on tours, paying for meals ashore, and are inclined to purchase things.

Large Ships Versus Smaller Ships

The size of the ship you choose can also impact your cruise significantly. For instance, larger ships generally have more activities and entertainment for families aboard than their smaller cousins. They also make for a more stable experience as they sail over waves rather than up and down them. Having said that, most modern cruise ships have stabilisers (these are fins that protrude out of the side of the ship) which do a great job of reducing the sideways rocking, and yawing motion of the ship.

As with anything, what is classed as an advantage in one respect can also be a disadvantage depending upon your specific requirements. For instance, the sheer size of some cruise ships can sometimes prevent them from mooring ashore at some ports. This means they have to anchor out at sea and use tenders to get passengers ashore. This can significantly reduce the time you spend ashore because you may find yourself in large queues waiting for a tender. If the sea is agitated, it can make the trip to the shore in a tender very unsteady and uncomfortable at times causing some people to feel seasick. The captain may even be forced to stop tenders going ashore altogether on occasions because of bad weather, meaning you might miss out on seeing certain ports altogether. Even if a large cruise ship can moor ashore, sometimes they are a long way from towns and cities because of their need for a deep water mooring.

If you think these aspects of cruising may be of concern to you, you can find out all of this information on cruise websites or in their brochures advertising your cruise. That is not to say all large cruise ships are required to moor offshore or miles from anywhere. Many more ports are able to accommodate the larger cruise ships because the draught/draft of many new ships is relatively shallow, and more effort has been made by ports to accommodate them – but it is worth checking this out if you think it might be an issue for you. Choosing a slightly smaller ship (25,000/40,000 Gross Tonnage opposed to 200,000 GT) can sometimes be more beneficial if visiting ports is your main focus. Smaller cruise ships also have a more intimate feel about them and you get to know crew and other passengers a little better.

Hurricane Season

Many people choose to cruise in hurricane season, (June to November in the Caribbean), or as it is called in other parts of the world, typhoon, tornado, and storm season. They do this because the cruises are generally cheaper, and there is plenty of sunshine. In addition to this, the infrastructure at ports in some of the Caribbean (St Thomas and St Martin for instance) is designed for very large cruise ships, and there are lots of sunny beaches close to the ports for people to relax on. This can ultimately mean less expense when at a port as tours and transport are often not required if your main desire is to relax on a beach and perhaps shop for the occasional souvenir. Statistics also suggest that the vast majority of cruises that sail at this time of the year do not come into contact with hurricanes at all. Even if a hurricane were to appear, modern cruise ships can often navigate around them. They can even out-run most hurricanes, as cruise ships generally travel over 20 knots, whilst hurricanes often travel only a little faster than a brisk walking pace.

But before you go ahead and book this cheaper option there are a few things to be mindful of. Cruise ships still need to sail through unsettled weather to get around or outrun hurricanes should they encounter one. This means you may expect at least some movement aboard from squally weather. You might be unlucky, and a hurricane is so severe your cruise is delayed, diverted, or even cancelled. Hurricane season also makes the weather more unpredictable, and it may rain rather heavily at times as weather fronts are moving around the oceans.

Whilst these issues may not be deal breakers for you, they are certainly worth keeping in mind, especially if you have never taken a cruise before. It would be a shame to be turned away from cruising entirely because of a bad first experience.

Repositioning Cruises

Repositioning cruises are another option you might consider. They are essentially called repositioning cruises because a ship is moving from one season of sailing to another – from Europe to the Caribbean for instance. They are often much cheaper than a standard cruise and are an excellent opportunity to see the less frequented cruise ship destinations. You can often book these cruises well in advance, and most cruise companies offer them.

Because repositioning cruises are generally a one-way trip, flights back home are often required – which can prove costly if not included in the cruise package deal. Try to get a repositioning cruise where flights are included or you might find any savings you have made are eaten up paying for air travel.

Tips

1. Taking a cruise in hurricane season is generally a cheaper option, and weather conditions are usually very favourable. But if you aren't prepared to miss ports because of bad weather, you might want to re-think your plans.
2. Don't think large ships don't rock and roll, they do, and especially in very bad weather. Despite stabilisers doing a great job, you can still have quite an unstable journey on very large ships if the weather is extremely bad. Having said that; on a typical cruise ships are stable, and people don't feel seasick.
3. When the ship is at port you can come and go as much as you like, and you can continue to use many of the facilities aboard. Some features of the ship may be closed when it is at port though, like the shops, and the casino for instance. There may also be limited youth facilities available.
4. Age and size of ship can make a distinct difference to your cruise. Some of the newer and larger ships have many more facilities, and a greater choice of shipboard activities.
5. Repositioning cruises are an excellent way to see some of the less frequented cruising destinations, and they are often a cheaper option. But the travel to or from the ship can prove expensive if not included in the deal.

3

Luggage Cases & Bags

On most cruise ships luggage weight isn't generally an issue if you are not flying to it, however, what cases and bags you take can affect your cruising experience quite considerably. If you don't want to be cuddling up to cases all night and building towers in the corners of your cabin, (which are often restricted for space) I highly recommend you think about what bags to take. My choice for many years has been a sports bag or climbing holdall - all be it a very good quality one with wheels. The benefit of using these kinds of bags is they have soft sides, flatten to almost nothing, and can be stored under the bed, in a wardrobe, and behind things. Yes, your clothes might get a little crumpled in transit, but when hung on a hanger or ironed they are perfectly good. If you have something that you feel is a little more precious, take it as hand luggage, or insert it in the centre of your clothes. You might also consider the Russian doll bags, as they have the advantage of being firm and secure, but pack neatly inside each other taking up little space in your cabin when empty.

Weight & Air Travel

I remember buying a case for an overseas trip, and on arriving at the airport I had to take virtually everything out of it because the bag itself was so heavy. I lugged that case around Spain, in and out of hotels, buses and trains carrying little more than a couple of pairs of underwear, and a toothbrush. Moral of this experience - if you are flying to a cruise make sure your case is lightweight because you might find you will be taking considerably less with you, or you may have to pay for the privilege of carrying something inside it.

Carry-On/Off-Bag – Cloth Bags

A carry-on/off bag is a small bag that holds a few essentials items in it, such as toiletries, a change of clothes, a swimming costume, and any other items you feel you will need when you don't have access to your luggage on a cruise ship. The carry-on/off bag is important to take because when you are on a cruise ship you may not have your luggage when you embark and disembark a ship for a substantial period of time.

Embarking - cruise companies will often take your cases and bags onto the ship and distribute them to cabins afterwards (this is generally when you have travelled by plane). This feature of cruising does, however, mean that you may have to wait for some time for your luggage to arrive in your cabin, as there may be thousands of bags for stewards to sort through on the ship. You can bypass this and take your own bags to your cabin in some circumstances, but it is often a heavy and a much less relaxing start to a cruise.

If you want to immediately start utilising the facilities aboard, or you simply want to change your cloths and freshen up properly, taking some essentials in a carry-on bag is a distinct benefit. If you pack a carry-on bag separately to your other luggage before leaving home it will also assist you if your luggage gets lost in transit on a plane (the cruise company will generally organize your bags to be sent to the next port if they get lost in transit). It is surprizing how often I have seen people without their luggage onboard because of issues with air-transport. You will, however, need to be aware of what toiletries you can pack inside a carry-on bag if you are going to use it for hand luggage on a plane, because liquids and aerosols have restrictions placed upon them when it comes to air travel.

Disembarking - on the penultimate day of your cruise your cases will need to be weighed and scanned prior to leaving the ship, which usually means you will be without your luggage from late afternoon. Having a carry-off bag means you can enjoy you cruise during this period, and you will be able to use the spa, have a swim, change your clothes, use your own toiletries and so forth. Make sure you remember to pack a set of clothes for the next day in it, as it has been known for some passengers to disembark in their pyjamas. Surprisingly, this is more common than you might think because many passengers pack their belongings in their cabin whilst wearing their PJ's, and sometimes they forget to leave clothes out for the next day. Once luggage has been taken to be sorted and scanned by the security department, you often can't get it back. Unfortunately, passengers can't even purchase anything suitable from the onboard shops the following morning, specifically if the ship is at port because commercial maritime laws often prevent any trading taking place.

Small cloth bags are perfect to use as a carry-on/off-bag because they have the added benefit of being versatile in allowing you to reuse them to carry purchases and such like throughout the cruise. It also means you are doing your bit for the environment as plastic bags have a tendency to blow off the ship and into the ocean. Many cruise passengers take small folding cloth bags with them on a cruise because their size means they can be carried in pockets and hand bags with ease, whilst still being able to carry large and heavy items inside.

Day Bags - Rucksack

Many passengers on cruise ships opt to take a small rucksack with them to carry essential items on tours. When I say they carry a rucksack, I don't mean they take a large rucksack with an internal frame that makes them look like they are going on an expedition to Everest; I mean they take one made of leather or material that looks quite stylish. The main advantage of these bags is that weight is distributed throughout your shoulders and your hands are free to take photographs and such like. Many passengers and crew also find them a little more secure than carrying bags in their hands, because bags can be left behind in places accidentally or snatched quite easily.

But even rucksacks have their downsides, especially when it comes to thieves in crowded locations. This is because in some countries thieves are waiting for cruise ships to arrive and are joining groups of passengers to steal what they can from them. Those engaging in this nefarious activity essentially stand behind people slicing rucksacks open, and stealing some of their contents without anyone being aware of what is happening. To reduce having important personal effects stolen this way, it is advisable to only take essential items with you ashore, and leave the rest in the safe inside your cabin (if you don't have a personal cabin safe, you can leave items in a safe at the Pursers desk). Don't place small valuable items in outer pockets or on the peripheries of your rucksack, as these are the main target places for thieves to slash open and steal their contents. If you are carrying something expensive like a camera, place it in the main body of your rucksack where you are more likely to feel someone tampering with it, or hang it around your neck ready to take shots. For any smaller items such as wallets, purses and passports, think about carrying a small bag close to your person.

Neck Wallets

To carry small items like passports, wallets, and money, people have traditionally used what are often termed as bum or fanny bags. They certainly keep important items close to your person, but they are often difficult to access under clothes, and make you look like an alien is about to emerge from your stomach. Many crew and regular cruise passengers are starting to use wallets that hang around the neck on a cord, and can be placed under your clothes but accessed very easily (many are also waterproof). Make sure you get a good quality one with secure zips and clips because the cheaper neck wallets don't take much abuse.

Tips

1. Soft fabric holdalls are good for carrying luggage if you don't mind getting your clothes a little crumpled. They can store under beds, behind wardrobes, and in many nooks and crannies in your cabin - think about getting ones with wheels though.
2. Carry-on/off-bags, keep essentials items available for embarking and disembarking when you don't have access to your cases. Use the same bag for other things such as purchases, carrying swimming ephemera and such like around with you.
3. Make sure your bags have strong tabs with your name and contact details on them because stickers can easily come off, which will ultimately add to the delay of you receiving your bags.
4. Handbag straps should be strong and long enough to go over your shoulder to stop them from being snatched by thieves.
5. Despite some countries being notorious for pick-pockets and thieves, make a habit of not leaving valuables in back pockets or on the peripheries of a rucksack every time you go ashore.
6. Neck wallets can be a great way to carry valuables because it makes them easily accessible to you, but under your clothes they are less accessible to thieves.
7. Place a few very small cloth bags that fold into a tiny package into your luggage, you will be surprised how handy they are around the ship.

4

What to Pack & Wear

The mistakes many passengers make when packing for a cruise is that they pack for it like they are packing for any other holiday/vacation, but it isn't any other holiday/vacation. Each cruise company has stipulations as to the dress code it requires for passengers - not to mention, you may be sailing through dramatically different climates, or visiting cultures where certain dress codes are required. Knowing what facilities are available, and what to expect onboard can also help you to be selective with what you take.

Prior to a cruise most cruise lines will send you literature or a link to a website highlighting the specifics of a cruise. Read through this information carefully so you can be sure of what to expect aboard. In the information you receive they will generally inform if there are any formal occasions aboard, and if so, what the acceptable attire for men, women, and children will be. It may also highlight what attire is appropriate for dining, swimming, relaxing on the decks, and the estimated temperatures for the different ports you will be visiting. This affords you the opportunity to pack appropriately, and reduces what you need to buy or hire whilst aboard.

Clothes Washing Facilities

On virtually all cruises, you will have access to clothes washing facilities through their onboard laundry department. Clothes are often washed, dried, and ironed in a day or two. Many cruise ships also have dry cleaning facilities, but the cost for cleaning each item is higher. If you feel you may be using the laundry regularly throughout a cruise you can purchase laundry packages, but they are often only available prior to a cruise.

Most cruise ships also have specific areas for passengers to do their own laundry, which can be a cheaper option, and a little more convenient for some (it is often a free service on larger ships, but you will have to pay for laundry detergent). The public laundry areas can get very congested at certain times of the day, generally after a port visit, late afternoon, or on sea days. There are, however, numerous self-service laundries on different levels of the ship, and a little searching may often reveal one that is not so congested. Alternatively, you could do your laundry when machines are less in demand, which is often early mornings, late evenings, port days and during formal events.

Be aware - if any of your clothes get damaged either by the ships laundry or washing them yourself you may not get any compensation. You should see terms and conditions to this affect in literature you receive before the cruise, or you may see notices in the laundry areas.

Cruise Dress Codes

Formal evenings are less of a feature on many cruise ships these days, but things haven't changed to the point of seeing topless bathing, and wet T-shirt competitions on all but the most liberal and party-oriented cruises, unless you stumble into a crew area by accident that is. But it certainly seems that things are becoming more casual in cruising. You may even find that shorts and T-shirts are acceptable for dining on some ships, although check first because some cruise companies that lean towards the casual cruiser still have dress codes for dining.

On the lido deck (pool deck) or just walking about the ship you can often wear what you like, but use a little discretion when going for meals because you may be asked to wear more than your swimming costume, and a pair of shorts in some restaurants that are open throughout the day. When going on tour excursions it is also appropriate to think about what you are wearing. Shorts and T-shirt are usually fine in most countries, but be aware of what slogans are on them as they can offend some cultures without you realising it (this is especially important if you are going to any religious buildings whilst ashore).

What to Take

Obviously, the type of cruise you decide to go on and where the cruise is going will determine much of what you will take, but here are some things you might want to consider before packing for a cruise.

General: you may be surprised how much walking you actually do on a cruise, so take shoes that are comfortable, work in a few environments, and are lightweight. Most cruise companies supply you with towels, shampoo, and soap, but if you have allergies or specific requirements, you might do well to take your own hair and body wash products.

Cold climates: people often make the mistake of packing only warm clothes for cruises that are going to cold climates. It is important to remember you will be on an air-conditioned ship, and will be able to comfortably wear what you want whilst aboard. You will also have access to heated or enclosed swimming pools, spas, and gyms.

You can also get burnt and dazzled by the sun in cold climates, especially if there is snow and ice, so take sun cream, and quality sunglasses with you.

Warm climates: with large numbers of people aboard some cruise ships (6000 plus), cruise lines often reduce air temperature aboard by a degree or two to combat germs spreading. This means the air conditioning in cabins can get rather chilly at times, and the same is true of some bus transport ashore. Take at least some warm clothing (sweater/cardigan) with you for these occasions. It is also a requirement to have warm clothes for any emergencies where you might need to board a lifeboat. You might also want to think about taking trousers that can turn into shorts, and garments that air dry quickly. Don't place clothes on outside verandas to dry because they can easily blow away into the ocean, which is both frustrating, and not very environmentally friendly.

Women: you can certainly wear shoes with heels including stilettoes aboard because all larger cruise ships are very stable. Wearing smart clothes or a dress for formal evenings is fine in most cases, although some cruise companies may ask for specific evening attire to be worn. If the ship has formal evenings, they usually only come into effect after 6 pm on certain designated nights.

Men: a quality suit or jacket with a shirt and coordinating shoes is often quite appropriate for formal occasions. You can sometimes hire formal clothes aboard, but check in the cruise literature first.

Children: taking additional clothes for children is probably more advantageous than it is for adults. Children often soil clothes much faster than adults and may require a few changes of clothes throughout the day. Most parents tell me that they pack extra swimming costumes and underwear for children. Children are also expected to be dressed appropriately if the ship has formal occasions, which would require bringing ties and suits for them.

My mantra when it comes to packing for a cruise is the acronym LAP - pack **less** than you think you need, pack **appropriately** for the ship and its itinerary, and pack for any additional **purchases** you may make.

Tips

1. Before a cruise, find out what dress codes are acceptable from the company website, as each ship and company have different standards and requirements.
2. If you don't like the whole formal approach, look for cruise companies that air on the casual side.
3. Be judicious in your packing because taking too much can mean being overweight if you are flying, but taking too little can mean more expense on your cruise as you will have to buy things.
4. Wet/damp garments are much heavier than dry ones, and if you are taking a flight it can make a substantial difference to what you can carry home.
5. Shoes are heavy, so think about taking ones that can work in a few environments, remembering you may be doing quite a lot of walking. Closed sandals are often great for many activities on the ship.
6. When ashore, be mindful of other cultures, try to respect their dress codes, and think of what slogans you have on T-shirts.
7. Washing machines and dryers are sometimes available in passenger areas (near passenger cabins) but if your clothes are damaged by the laundry department, you may not get any compensation.
8. Children often require more clothes than adults, and taking changes of clothes and warm clothes for them on tour excursions is a good idea.

5

Gratuity

Not all cruise companies have a gratuity system, but at the moment the majority do. Each cruise company adopts a specific way for passengers to pay for gratuity. Some cruise companies provide envelopes in each cabin on the penultimate day of the cruise for passengers to deposit money into. This method for paying gratuity was very common on cruise ships at one time, but over recent years' other methods have become more popular.

With some cruise companies you will have gratuity taken out of your onboard account over the course of a cruise as a daily surcharge. With others, you will be expected to pay the gratuity before a cruise (at the time of booking) and sometimes you cannot even book a cruise unless you pay gratuity with the initial payment.

Before committing to any cruise, it is worth finding out exactly what the gratuity charge will be because it can fluctuate considerably between companies, and the cabin category that you choose. Children are often not excluded from this surcharge, so make sure if you are booking a cruise for the family that you account for this as well. It may work out that your cruise might not be the bargain you initially thought it was when you factor gratuity into the price.

With some cruise companies you can request a partial or complete refund for any gratuities paid, but this is entirely at the discretion of the cruise company. Generally, this can only be dealt with by the pursers' desk when you are aboard the ship. Some passengers request, or at least try to request a refund of any gratuities paid because they prefer to choose what crewmembers they want their money to go to, rather than have the cruise company make the decision for them. They see it as a way to individually reward someone for going above and beyond in service.

Whilst this may seem a plausible and valid approach, there is one problem in doing it. The gratuity charge for a cruise is often designed to pay the wages of all the service sector (or is supposed to be). By giving your gratuity to a select few crewmembers who are dealing with you face to face, you would be depriving other crewmembers behind the scenes of what is rightfully their share.

Double/Triple Tipping & Skewed Service

The tipping culture on cruise ships has caused uncertainty and confusion for many years because passengers were often not sure who to tip, what to tip, and when to tip. Many passengers also felt like they would only get good service if they did tip. It could be argued that paying gratuity ultimately stops any concerns passengers have about tipping. This is because when you pay gratuity you have effectively given one payment for services onboard, thus overriding the need to offer a tip for good service. Gratuity also has a distinct benefit for crewmembers because they will be assured a regular wage, which they wouldn't necessarily have received from tips because they are based upon the generosity of others, and therefore can fluctuate with every cruise.

A win-win for all – well not quite.

Whilst the gratuity system might allay any concerns passengers and crew have about tipping, it certainly could appear to be making what was once considered a generous gift into a compulsory payment. Added to this, tipping seems so ingrained into cruise culture, even with gratuity being taken out of passengers accounts, many people still feel obliged to tip for service. Added to this, many crewmembers seem to expect a tip despite the gratuity system. If one subscribes to the dictionaries definition of gratuity – *a generous gift for good service* or something similar, you will essentially be double tipping if you do this.

You may even find yourself triple tipping when you pay for certain things aboard, like a drink from the bar for instance. This is because a chit brought with a drink may well ask you to sign for an extra gratuity to be given for that particular service. If you then decide to hand over a dollar to the steward, you have effectively paid 3 tips – the gratuity for the cruise service sector as a whole, a gratuity for the specific drink to be brought to you, and a tip to the steward for bringing it. This double/triple tip payment means not only are you paying even more for a cruise if you double/triple tip, you may not get the service of others that do double/triple tip if you don't double/triple tip – if you know what I mean. It could also mean that cruise companies might stop giving the gratuity to crewmembers because they believe they are getting adequate remuneration from tips off passengers.

Unlike a tip, gratuity is distributed to crewmembers irrespective of the quality of service they provide and doesn't incentivise excellent service – or at least it doesn't seem to. It is not surprising I suppose that some passengers get irritated by the gratuity charge because it seems to create a cloak and mirror approach to charging properly for a cruise. With this in mind one could reasonably ask - is gratuity worth keeping in the cruise industry, and wouldn't a standard price for the whole cruise be far simpler?

Whatever way you look at it, paying gratuity is not a simple solution to avoiding paying tips, incentivising crewmembers, or indeed paying the wage of a section of the crew. It might initially make a cruise look cheaper, but in the process it can make a passenger feel like the cruise company are not being entirely forthcoming with the true charge of a cruise.

With all that said, whilst you might not be completely happy with certain aspects of how the price of a cruise is arrived at, if it offers a competitive price, (taking into account gratuity, and the occasional tip) then ultimately it is a good deal. If you are particularly irritated about gratuity or tipping on cruise ships, you can look for companies that don't have it, (there are some out there I believe) or you could register your complaints about it on comment cards when you get aboard cruise ships that subscribe to gratuity and tipping. You can also write a review on most company's website about aspects you thought could be improved. With more people organizing their vacation around reviews these days, companies are paying more attention to suggestions people make.

One thing is for sure. If you have booked a cruise, which includes gratuity and tipping, it would be a shame not to enjoy it thoroughly despite your personal opinions.

Tips

1. Gratuity is a daily charge that will be added to your cruise account. It is quite common on cruise ships and should pay the wages of a section of the crew. Be aware of how much gratuity will be deducted so you can budget for it. The price of the cruise and the cabin you choose can also determine how much you pay.
2. Not all cruises companies work on the gratuity system, but most do.
3. Some passengers have expressed concerns that the gratuity taken from them simply goes to the company, and not to the individual crewmembers. If this is a concern, inquire about this prior to your cruise by contacting the company, or look at their literature.
4. Gratuity accounts are set up on most cruise ships to take money from passengers for services. This charge may or may not be added to all-inclusive package deals.
5. Opting out of having gratuity taken out of your account is possible, but makes it difficult for the passenger to be sure they have adequately paid for all the services they have received from the crew.
6. If you have a complaint about the tipping culture on cruise ships, tell the cruise company and not the staff that are serving you. Complaining to staff cannot change anything, and besides, they are doing their best to serve you under the conditions imposed upon them.

6

Tipping

Whilst you are on a cruise you may find yourself needing or indeed wanting to tip because of the excellent service you have received from crewmembers. I may also be that no gratuity is taken from your account, and you are expected to leave a tip to pay for the service you have received. Whatever your reason for tipping on a cruise, I will 'try' to explain how to get your head around it should you wish to do it, and help you get an idea of what an appropriate tip would be in certain circumstances.

I will also be addressing why tipping is so problematic when it comes to paying for services onboard. You may have noticed I place emphasis on the word try. This is because I believe giving a concrete answer is very difficult as so many factors can effect what tip is given. Hence, you may notice I am occasionally vague, and sometimes resort to humour. This perhaps highlights tipping's key attribute – it is more confusing than trying to work out the instruction manual for flat pack furniture when written in a foreign language.

Who to Tip

The service sector is the main area you have to think about when it comes to tipping. This includes waiters, cleaners, room stewards, bar staff and such like. Those providing spa treatments, massages, hairdressing and so forth may also require a tip. They are often not part of the group who benefit from the gratuity taken out of your account, as they generally work for an outside company. Some of these workers (although certainly not all) do not get a wage and are solely reliant upon any tips given. They may get a percentage rate of any treatments, products bought, or even a small wage, but this can sometimes mean they take very little money home. Tipping can sometimes be the only way many of these people get a decent income.

How Much to Tip

How much you tip is very dependent upon what service you have been provided. For instance, if it is a waiter bringing you a drink, then it could be a simple as handing a dollar or two over to them. If it is a driver taking you somewhere, or someone serving you a meal, it might be a case of working out a rough percentage rate of the total figure, with 10%, 15% or even 20% being standard for a tip.

Things become more complex when it comes to deciding how much to pay your cabin steward because there is no fixed price to work out a percentage with. In this situation you could perhaps ask another passenger what they pay as a tip to their cabin steward or waiter; but in order to get a balanced and fair account of how much you should pay, it might be appropriate to ask quite a few people a variety of questions. This is because some passengers are more generous than others, and some have bigger cabins than others. (A larger tip is generally expected from those in suites and larger cabins, as more work is done by the room steward and other departments on the ship.)

The following paragraph may seem a little ad absurdum when it comes to explaining what an appropriate tip may be in some circumstances, but it highlights the critical problems I see with tipping.

In a desire to assess what a fair tip would be for a cabin steward, you might actually be required to run through a questionnaire with other passengers asking questions such as, how large is your cabin, and how generous would you rate yourself on a scale of 1 to 10? Would you base your stewards time and effort worthy of a similar wage to your own – please provide your annual salary including any bonuses for the past 5 years, and explain in 250 words what you would pay and why. Once you have assessed the average from all of these passengers, you can then start to form your own opinions on what tip would be appropriate to leave.

Failing this method, you could always do some research on what a decent monthly wage would be for a person in a cabin stewards position, and divide it by how many cabins they looked after.

Perhaps you don't want to work that hard on a cruise, and you realise your calculations aren't as good as you would like them to be having consumed vast amounts food and alcohol whilst aboard. If this is how you feel my advice would be; if you are paying gratuity don't worry about how much you tip, or whether you should tip because if you decide to tip for exceptional service whatever you tip is a bonus. If no gratuity is taken out of your cruise costs –

please insert your own suggestion if mine is not appropriate, as I can't give you any more advice in this instance ....

....

....

....

Why Tipping is Problematic

The problem with tipping is, most people like to know what they are paying for and budget for it accordingly. Yes, they might like to show their gratitude on occasions, but if that gratitude is expected and frowned upon when not displayed or insufficient, it can cause issues. The other problem with tipping is, the parameters are constantly changing depending upon what cabin a passenger is in, and the level of service that is given. In addition to this, everyone is reliant upon someone else's notion of what generosity is. Hence, there is no simple answer to the question – how much should I tip?

Tipping also creates a climate of uncertainty, as crewmembers don't know exactly what they will be taking home, and passengers are not sure what the overall cost of a cruise will be. Some crewmembers may say that they like the tipping culture because it means they sometimes take more money home than they expected, but it is a different story when the tips aren't forthcoming. Some passengers may say that tipping people makes them feel good about themselves and others around them because they are rewarding someone for going above and beyond standard service. But the same actions could also demonstrate a desire to curry favour, buying gratitude, and generally blurring the lines of showing appreciation and conveying a controlling power over others. In my experience, tipping often creates a distorted way for crew to view passengers, and passengers to view crew.

If you are on a ship that has tipping, all I can say is - good luck with your questionnaires and calculations. May your stress levels stay low, your goodwill to others be apportioned appropriately, and your bank balance stay healthy.

Tips

1. Standard tip and gratuity charges are anywhere between 10% and 20%.
2. Don't feel obliged to tip if gratuity is taken from your account.
3. If you are going to tip, carry small change with you, and often dollars are accepted on all cruise ships whatever nationality it is.
4. If you are not paying gratuity, you may find envelopes on your bed to deposit tips for crewmembers.
5. Gratuities deducted by a company can vary considerably, and it can take a little searching to find out what each company charges.
6. Asking other passengers is a great way to find out what to tip, but be mindful of how generous they are, and what category of cabin they are in, as this can affect how much they tip.
7. You can also ask crewmembers how much to tip, but use some common sense when determining what their motives are.
8. Tipping is not an exact science, so try and use your common sense when it comes to how much to give.
9. There are cruise companies out there that do not have a tipping culture.

7

Tours

Most of the tours the cruise companies provide are run by independent operators, but they source the companies that they feel will offer the quality and service that fits their cruise clientele. They regularly send out staff to monitor tours, and any constructive criticism is generally taken seriously, and dealt with promptly.

As you can imagine, if you organise and book tours yourself without going through the cruise company, it can often be a substantially cheaper option as the cruise surcharge is not placed on top of the tour. But it also means you may have to make your own way to where a tour is departing, rather than being picked up at the cruise terminal as with cruise organised tours. This may sound like a trivial point but it can be difficult to get to some destinations to meet for a tour from certain ports, especially if the port is very large, or is miles away from anywhere. I have seen many passengers miss private tours because of this, and they often are not able to obtain a refund.

If you decide to book your own tour excursion, it is important to do your homework to make sure you can arrive at their assigned meeting point at the agreed time. Find out as much as you can about the port, and the local area in advance, so you know what to expect before you arrive. You may even be able to get someone to pick you up in the port, but this may not be possible for some external tour operators because permits and passes may be needed to get access onto port areas.

It is also important to make sure that the tour operator/operators you are using are licenced properly. In some countries unlicensed tour operators may not place safety as a priority on the tour. The other thing to be aware of with booking your own tour is, the ship will not wait for you to return if your tour is running late. Booking on a cruise organised tour means, even if the tour gets held up, the ship will wait for it to return. This can be a distinct advantage in some countries were traffic is traditionally bad, and you might get held up for many hours.

Booking Cruise Tours

Cruise organised tours are always very popular, and they generally fill up incredibly quickly despite often being more expensive than organising your own. You can book cruise tours at the time of booking your cruise with most companies, but many passengers still seem to wait until they arrive onboard to do it. On some cruise ships you can even book your tour through a mobile app or on your cabin television, meaning you don't even need to get out of bed to do this if you don't want to.

If you haven't pre-booked your tour, pick up a brochure from the tour excursions office when you first arrive aboard, and book your excursions as soon as you can. Your punctuality will be rewarded, and you won't be left having to go on a tour of the local sewage factory because that is all that was left by the time you booked it.

Cancelling a Cruise Tour and Cancellations

If you decide to change your mind about a tour at a later date you can generally cancel 24/48 hours before it departs without losing any money. However, if you pre-book a tour at the time of booking you may incur a fee with some cruise companies if you cancel a tour at any time throughout a cruise. (Cancellation policies vary between companies, so check what each cruise company's policy is in regards to cancellations and refunds before you book any tours.)

If you find some of the tours are already full when you arrive aboard, you can ask to be placed on a cancellation list as people often change their minds. If your tour is cancelled, the tour department will often do their best to offer an alternative. They may even offer a partial refund for the inconvenience of this, whilst still providing another tour.

Where do Cruise Tours Depart from?

If you want to know more about a particular tour before booking it, you will find a full detailed explanation of each tour at the shore excursions department. Make sure you pay particular attention to where, and at what time the tour will be departing because they generally don't wait for more than a few minutes for passengers that are running late. This may sound like an obvious point, but tours meet in different places, and just because one tour met in a certain place the previous day, it doesn't mean another tour will do the same the following day. Many passengers have missed a tour because of going to the wrong meeting place, or by having the incorrect time for departure.

If you are meeting for a tour that is departing in the morning or you are taking a tender to the shore, it is a good possibility you will be required to congregate in a large room aboard the ship (a theatre or something similar). You may be given an identifying sticker or wristband, and will generally be asked to sit in certain sections with others going on the same tour. By doing this, there are fewer chances passengers will miss their tour by waiting in long queues as others try to exit the ship. This process can be a little frustrating at times because you may arrive at the meeting place at the requested time, but find yourself spending an hour or so sitting around on the ship waiting with many others for your tour to leave.

Tours & Food

In some countries sourcing food yourself can be difficult. This is because vegetables are sometimes washed in polluted water, fruits (including those with skins) are left in rivers to absorb polluted water to swell their size, drinks can be made from powders and polluted water, and the hygiene engaged by those preparing foods may not be the most rigorous. Cruise companies only use tour operators that pass their stringent quality controls, and it might be worth the added expense to include a tour with food and drink in some countries where you can't be sure of its quality.

To keep things cheap, you may decide to take a packed lunch with you from the ship, but make sure before doing this that it is permitted by the local authorities and the cruise line. This is because some countries will not allow certain foodstuffs to be taken off the ship, unless hermetically sealed. Bottled water on the other hand can be expensive, and there is generally no problem with taking your own on the tour as long as it is sealed when leaving the ship.

Tips

1. Cancelling cruise tours is possible with many cruise lines, but there will be a cut off time for this, which is usually 24 or 48 hours before a tours departure. If you pay for a tour at the time of booking your cruise, you may incur a charge even if you cancel within the stipulated period.
2. Tour meeting places are often in theatres and other large spaces on the ship. They may also be at an outside location especially if it is an afternoon tour.
3. Missing a tour might not be as big a catastrophe as you imagine. Similar tours may be leaving, and you might be able to get on another one. You can also take a taxi to join them if you ask the tour department where their first stop is going to be. Missing the tour generally means you will not get a refund.
4. Taking food off the ship is not permitted on some cruise lines and in certain ports. This is especially the case if it is not sealed hermetically.
5. Half day tours are great if you want to break up the day, and you can have some relaxation whilst still seeing something of the area.
6. Take something warm with you on tour, as the air-conditioning in coaches can be cold.
7. Try to keep valuables on you at all times when on a tour, leaving only none valuable items on the bus.

8

Cruise Tours (Types of Tours)

In this chapter, I am going to look at what to expect when you book tours through the cruise company. This is certainly not a definitive list of the types of tours you will encounter, but it will give you an idea what to expect on some of the most common cruise tours.

Sightseeing/Shopping Tours

Sightseeing tours are the most popular tours provided by cruise companies. This is perhaps because they generally give passengers a good overview of an area. They are also an easy and comfortable way to see places, and you can expect the guide to be knowledgeable, and speak good English or a language you understand - accents can sometimes be a challenge with some tour guides at times.

Being a part of a large group that is walking about together can at times seem like you are waving a red flag to a bull in attracting local sales people. They can get rather persistent in wanting you to buy their wares in some countries, so expect a little more attention from sales people.

Be careful to read the descriptions of sightseeing tours carefully, and focus on any tell-tale signs of shopping. I say this because whilst the title of the tour may sound fantastic - '*A Cultural Introduction of Alexandria - experience the city as a local, and understand what it is like to be in some of the oldest and most vibrant parts of this ancient culture.*' In reality the tour description should have read – 'we are going to take you to a bunch of shops and markets where you will be pestered to death to buy a load of old tat.' Whilst most tours offer some shopping so you can purchase a memento or gift, a genuine sightseeing tour should not have shopping as its key feature. If shopping is what you want, many cruise companies offer this as a genuine tour option – there is no accounting for taste I suppose! You may, however, find on these shopping tours, that they only take you to places they approve of – which can be limiting when it comes to choice.

Bus Tours

Bus tours generally allow passengers to explore more places of interest in the one day, which makes them very popular. The cruise companies generally make sure the transport is of a very high standard, with air conditioning and onboard toilets - although not always. I have taken cruise organised tours in the Amazon, Ecuador, Panama and Columbia to name a few, and the busses looked like they were built in 1910 and were recently retrieved from a scrap yard, but that is not the norm.

If the bus doesn't have toilets, you may find that a lot of time is taken up with toilet stops, depending upon the age and infirmity of the other passengers. Taking stops with 30 or 40 people is never a quick event, and invariably one person doesn't listen to the instructions and keeps everybody waiting whilst they have a cup of coffee or haggle a deal for an item they want to purchase. It might actually be that you find yourself spending a substantial amount of time waiting around.

If you are not accustomed to traveling on buses for long periods, you could also feel a little unwell by being cocooned on one all day. This might be because you are sat at the back of the bus, and the only air you get comes from a blower providing a stale breeze on your head. If you do feel sick on bus travel make a request to the tour guide or when booking the tour for a seat near the front of the bus, (being at the front of the bus seems to reduce the feeling of nausea for many people) and explain why you are asking for it. Also, make sure you arrive for the tour early to be sure of getting your requested seat.

If you are the kind of person that wants to see as much of an area as you can, or you feel unusually irritated waiting around for others, or perhaps you just want to have a more personalised experience, then you might want to think twice about taking a bus tour. If on the other hand you want to have a chat with fellow passengers, and like the thought of experiencing an area in a relaxing air-conditioned environment, then bus tours are a fantastic choice.

Drop-Off Tours

Some of the cruise ship destinations may have multiple ships in port at once, and it often works out that thousands of passengers are trying to acquire local transport at the same time. As you can imagine there is only so much transport to go around, so many passengers struggle to find private a taxi to take them to local cities or places of interest. A drop off tour is one where the cruise company organises to take passengers to a place, (such as a town, city, beach, or place of interest) and arranges a time and place for them to be picked up. The cruise companies may charge a premium for this facility, but it might be worth the additional expense in busy ports.

These tours are also very good if the ship is moored in the middle of nowhere because they can make local towns or cities much more accessible, whilst having guaranteed transport to return you to the ship. Drop-off tours can help to reduce the stress you may encounter in certain locations because you will be assured of transport back to the ship. It also means, if for some reason the transport was delayed in getting back to the ship, the captain would wait for it to return.

Bespoke Tours

Many cruise companies are trying to make the tour experience for passengers more bespoke these days, and are providing alternative tours for the more adventurous, such as zip lining, white water rafting, coast steering and such like. (Make sure your insurance covers you for the more extreme activities if you are going to do them on a cruise, as these can be add-ons to vacation insurance policies. Failure to cover yourself specifically for these kind of activities could mean you are not insured if you have an accident.)

The amount of activity tours you will have to choose from on a cruise is often determined by the kind of passenger the cruise company is trying to market and appeal to. If you are on a cruise that is designed to appeal to younger people and families, you can expect more activity tours to choose from at the tour excursions department.

Many cruise lines are also keen to differentiate themselves from other land-based operators they don't work with. They liaise with their partner operators to make tours very distinct and different from anything else that may be provided by the local tour operators. You might have a tour that lasts for several hours, but includes bus, boat, and a meal; with a few additional activities thrown in for good measure.

Whatever tour you choose, read the tour description thoroughly, and if you have any questions, always ask the team at the tour department. Chances are, they have already been on the tour themselves, and can tell you exactly what to expect.

Tips

1. Many cruise ships have a dedicated port lecturer who explains what to expect at each destination. They will often give you transport options, where banks are located, and other essential information. These talks often take place in the evenings before a port is visited, and can be seen in the theatre, or on your cabin TV.
2. Sickness can be common at the back of a bus, and it also takes much longer to get on and off from the back unless there are multiple exit/entrances.
3. Drop-off tours are quite common on some cruise ships, and they can give you the freedom to explore knowing you have transport to get back to the ship – but it can often be done much cheaper on your own.
4. Shopping tours can often be hard to identify, and good money can be spent on a tour that does not suit your requirements. Make sure you read all the descriptions carefully before booking a tour, and ask the tour staff if you are unsure.
5. Tours can fill very quickly, so book them as early as possible.
6. If you leave something on a bus or tour, contact the shore excursions team, and they will get in touch with the tour operator who will try to return it to the ship before it departs.
7. Make sure your insurance covers you for the more extreme activities if you are going to do them on a cruise.

9

Organising Your Own Tour

If you are going to organise your own tour for either some or all of the ports visited, the more time you take reading about each area the ship will be stopping at, the better equipped you will be when you get there. Knowing where the cruise will be stopping in relation to towns and cities, and what the local transport is like, also allows you to choose the destinations that will be better suited to exploring places yourself.

Some cruise brochures and websites (like the ones you get from travel agents) include detailed maps of where the ship will be docking in relation to towns and cities. They will sometimes even give you estimated walking/transport times from the ship to places of interest.

Booking in Advance

Many people book a tour in advance of a cruise with an independent operator, so that when they arrive at a port they have everything organised. Despite it being a cheaper option than booking through the cruise company, there are some things you need to be mindful of before doing it. For instance, you can't check the weather will be good for the activity weeks or months in advance. Irrespective of conditions, you may be expected to go on the tour or lose your deposit (or the full amount) if you don't attend. On a cruise organised tour, you can generally cancel or swap a tour a few days before the excursion without losing any money. The other issue with booking your own excursions in advance is; if tenders are required to go ashore from the cruise ship, and the weather does not permit them to be launched, it could mean losing your deposit as you can not get to the excursion you have booked. Booking in advance through external operators means, no matter how genuine and trustworthy they are, it does not guarantee you will get a refund, or indeed any money back if you change your mind, or miss the tour for whatever reason.

Booking On the Day

Booking a tour on the day you arrive at a port obviously stops any possibility of you losing your deposit, and you can also book an excursion based on the weather (cruise ships often have a dedicated weather channel). It also means that you can engage a taxi driver, a hire company, or local bus at your whim, and make your day as bespoke as you like.

There are a few options you can choose when it comes to booking transport, and the remainder of this chapter looks at some of the most popular ones.

Taxi Cabs

This seems to be the most popular way for independent cruise travellers to get about in many ports because they can leave it to someone else who knows the area, roads, and traffic to do the driving. Taxis can often be inexpensive to hire in some countries, and there is an immediacy about them, whilst bringing flexibility in where you go. Despite their obvious advantages they can prove problematic, and here are some suggestions you might find useful if you decide to organise your own cab.

Haggle a flat fee, even if the driver says that they are on a meter you can always go to another cab driver and see if they will do it for you. Get a few quotes because this helps you get the correct price and not some over-inflated one they sometimes offer cruise passengers. Don't let a cab driver offer you a cheap deal if they can take you to some of their favourite places. These places will invariably be shops charging exorbitant prices with the heavy sell included when you get there. Pick a driver that understands some English (or your own language) as you can often find yourself miles from where you wanted to be, and struggling to get back to where you came from because you can't communicate. Don't let a driver see your cash or how much you have, it can be too much temptation for some of them. In all countries, roadwork's, traffic jams, and accidents can hold you up; so if the driver gives you a time they will arrive back at the ship, add on a substantial amount of time for any unforeseen occurrences. Finally, never leave anything valuable in a cab, even if it is for a short time whilst you take a photograph because drivers have been known on more than one occasion to drive off with your valuables inside.

Local Busses

Local buses can be a fantastic way to see a city or a country, and are often very inexpensive, but they do have their drawbacks. Due to language issues, it can be difficult to get the exact bus you require, which can be a real problem if you are trying to get back to the ship. Added to this, they don't always keep to schedules or times. Busses are also some of the favourite places for pickpockets to frequent, so keep any items close to your person at all times.

Hiring – Bikes, Motorbikes and Cars

Make sure you take your licence before you think about hiring motorised transport – you don't necessarily need an international licence for this. Be careful of leaving your licence with some operators; due to identity theft, some of them ask to keep passports and licences, and use them for nefarious purposes. (Make a few photocopies of your licence and passport before leaving home so you can leave them with rental companies because many don't have photocopy facilities - try not to leave originals.)

Road rules, traffic conditions and the vehicle you are driving may be unfamiliar to you, (even bicycles) so it is important to make sure you understand the local laws. Roads in many countries are also uneven and sandy, and whilst locals make riding a motorbike look easy carrying 3 people, a cow and half their house as pillion, you probably will not. Motorbikes are one of the most common causes of serious accidents and deaths of tourists. (As is the case with extreme activities, make sure your insurance covers you for motorcycles, quad bikes and jet skies etc. as these can be add-ons to vacation insurance policies.)

Areas you have never been to before can often look the same, and if you can't read signs because of language issues, it is very easy to get lost. Buying a quality local map, downloading street maps, or just having a satellite image on your phone of each area allows you to see where you are in regards to the port. It is always easier to point to an image for directions from locals if there are language issues. (Satnav's are also a good idea, or downloading satnav app's to your mobile.) Missing the ship in a foreign country can be expensive and very stressful.

People who take cruises regularly often stand in two distinct groups. One group tells you that organising tours yourself is the best option because cruise companies are trying to rip you off on their tours. The other group will tell you that they only feel confident of having a safe and relaxing tour when they book through the cruise company. They also feel they are guaranteed a quality guide, great food, good transport, and that the ship will wait for them to return. So which is one is right?

We all have different approaches to things, and what one person sees as simple to organise might not be what another feels relaxed doing. Do what you feel comfortable with, and is within your budget, remembering the objective is to enjoy the cruise, and not just to save money. You may find it advantageous to mix things up a little by booking organised tours for some ports, and doing your own thing in others.

Tips

1. Having a map of the area on your mobile or a physical one is often a big help if you get lost. Downloading any maps before leaving home is a good idea, as it can be expensive to download on the ship because of Wi-Fi charges. Having a map allows you to point to where you need to go if you can not communicate in any other way.
2. Don't display expensive equipment because in some countries simply showing a camera can attract unwanted attention.
3. Asking crewmembers for good ways to get about certain ports is always a good idea. This is because they have probably been there numerous times before, and know all the scams, or at least have heard about them on the crew grapevine.
4. Don't get overly friendly with cab drivers because they see cruise passengers as an opportunity to substantially increase the fare, and being too friendly encourages them to ask for more money.
5. Hiring motorbikes might seem a cheap option, but sometimes a little more money could mean you get a car, which is certainly a safer option in a place you don't know.
6. Taking a cab can often be the cheapest and safest option of all in some countries.
7. Photocopies of licences and passports are always good to carry with you because some companies don't have facilities to copy your documents.

10

Food (Inclusive)

Food is something that features 'heavily' on most cruises, and sometimes the sheer quantity and quality of it can become a little over tantalising at first. The fact that much of this deliriously, delectable food is generally part of your inclusive payment, just adds to the temptation to indulge. You can eat to your heart's content on most cruises without having to pay anything to have a gastronomical feast. This is certainly good news if you are budget conscious, and perhaps bad news if you are worried about putting on weight. There are exceptions to what you can eat for free, and some cruises charge you for every meal aboard, but they are few and far between. Generally, when you book a cruise, plenty of food is included in the price with a very good selection to choose from. This is not to say that all food and drink aboard will be free or inclusive, you can expect to pay for some, which I will discuss in the next chapter.

Inclusive Restaurant/Dining Area

As a passenger, part of your traditional inclusive experience is to be allocated a dining station, a table, and a time to eat main meals - unless you are on a cruise that subscribes to flexi dining that is. Flexi dining is becoming more popular with cruise companies in recent years, and it simply means you have more flexibility in what table and time you choose to eat. Some cruises have even dispensed with the main dining area, and you have your evening meal at smaller themed restaurants, although this is not common to most cruise ships at the moment. For the most part, when it comes to inclusive meals you will be given a choice of 2 times to dine, either first or second sitting (the first sitting is generally around 6pm and the second is around 8pm). When you have agreed to a specific sitting, you generally have to keep to that timeslot for the duration of the cruise.

The dining experience at these meals is of a banquet style with a few courses, and you could be sharing this experience with anywhere up to 10 (or even more) other diners on some ships. You will generally have the same stewards and dining partners throughout your cruise. Whilst it is all well and good getting to know your fellow passengers and crew on the larger tables, it can sometimes wear thin if you are sharing a table with an irritating person/persons. There are a few of things you can do to combat this situation, and you could reach over the table pick up their lobster, and slap them over the head with it (shrimps and other crustaceans don't work quite as well). If this approach sounds slightly inappropriate, (I certainly would not recommend it, and it would be a waste of quality food) you can also ask to move tables, but this may not always be possible, so you might need to pay for a meal or eat in the buffet. If you miss your allocated sitting for whatever reason, or you don't find yourself feeling hungry and miss your allocated meal sitting, you will generally have to make alternative meal arrangements yourself.

Breakfast & Lunch

Breakfast and lunch (depending on the cruise company) is generally included in the price of your cruise, and is often in the same venue as your evening meal. Unlike the evening meal, however, breakfast or lunch is generally open seating, and you can sit at any table.

The Buffet

The buffet is very much an area where you can be casual and relax. As its name suggests, you are not served by stewards, but collect food and take it to a table of your choosing. On many ships there are no buffet dress codes and you can turn up with you bathing suit on if you like, but some cruise lines expect a certain level of attire (a sarong over a bathing suit, or shorts and a T-shirt, that sort of thing).

The buffet is generally an inclusive food venue and is positioned near the lido deck (top pool deck). It is always a good option for a quality choice of food throughout the day, and late into the evening. If you are a vegetarian for instance, as I was for a few years, the buffet is your go-to place. This is because it has an assortment of salads and green vegetables, and a host of other none meat products. (As well as having a large choice for none vegetarians of course.)

The food is also of an outstanding quality, and you could easily eat here for the whole cruise without a problem. It is open 24/7 on many ships, although there are times when sections are cordoned off for cleaning, or for a change of menus. The choice of food is also much larger throughout the day than in the early hours of the morning, or at comfort food times.

The buffet has its staples, which are available whenever you go, but it also varies what is available throughout the cruise so no two days will have all the same selection. This is because many cruise lines have themed days such as Hawaiian, Caribbean, Island, Mediterranean, and so forth.

Other Free Food

When people book a cruise through their future cruise operator, as a gesture of goodwill they may be offered a speciality meal for free (these are often at onboard restaurants you would normally pay for). You may also see other bonus meals being thrown in for free at the time of booking a cruise, and even if they aren't, ask for them - travel agents often have little incentives they can throw in for free.

But there are many other ways you can eat for free on a cruise outside of your allotted dining times – as long as you are prepared to be that little bit savvy. (For the pedantic among you, I do appreciate no food is truly free on a cruise ship, because you paid for food when you purchased the cruise, it just becomes cheaper the more you eat.) You can often eat at the poolside grill, pizza parlours, and soft serve ice-cream venues for free. Sometimes you will have to go at certain times of the day to get it free, and those times will often be advertised in leaflets left in your cabin. Many of the cruise organised functions also supply substantial nibbles. You can often get cabin service for free, although check first. If you go to a bar at certain times of the day or evening they also hand out food for free, such as finger food and dips. Many cruise lines are also including special afternoon tea areas with an award-winning master pâtissier making some of the most amazing deserts you can imagine.

I can hear some of you thinking (or indeed saying) whilst reading this section, 'what is the point in identifying all these places to eat for free when you generally have 3 main meals as part of your all-inclusive deal, not to mention the many other places to snack for free?' I mention them simply because they provide you with more choice and variety aboard. This is particularly important if you are on a slightly longer cruise because it breaks things up a little, and just adds to the overall experience.

Tips

1. For any dietary stipulations you have, contact the cruise company in advance to make arrangements for your needs. You can often highlight your dietary requirements when you arrive onboard, but it may take a while before you stop getting the wrong foods.
2. If you know you will not be attending the meal at your inclusive dining table for whatever reason, it is a good idea to tell the cruise personnel (Maitre-D). It means that other passengers on that table can arrange for someone to join them if they want.
3. Themed buffet nights can be a real opportunity to sample food from different cultures. They also may have a party on the deck with free alcohol on some occasions.
4. Confrontation on dining tables can happen with obstreperous dining partners. If someone is ruining your meal because of their talk, or attitude, you can ask to be repositioned or given another time slot; but it isn't always possible to do. Some passengers who are keen to get another timeslot may swap with you, but always organise this with the cruise personnel.
5. Ice-creams can be free at certain times of the day, and it might be real dairy ice-cream, and not soft serve.
6. Cabin service can be free on many cruise ships.

11

Food (None Inclusive)

Whilst looking for additional venues to get food for free might sound bizarre to some of your reading the last chapter, it might come as even more of a surprise to know that many passengers regularly buy food and meals aboard. I can hear you ask, 'why would anyone pay for additional food when they have already paid for food as part of their inclusive deal?

Perhaps the most common reason for passengers wanting to pay for a meal is, it provides them with the opportunity to have an intimate meal with their loved one/ones, and it gives them a larger choice. Pushing the boat - or should that be the ship out a little, and spending extra on an intimate meal, can make for a more memorable occasion, and cruise. It might surprise those who have never taken a cruise to hear that most cruise lines have plenty of speciality restaurants that are full of passengers eagerly paying for their meals. Speciality restaurants can be so busy at times you can struggle to get a table in them, and you might even be forced to book well in advance, or only be able to dine in them once. On most cruises, however, there is no limit to the number of times you can eat in speciality restaurants, and the choices you have are extensive. Passengers in suites, and more expensive apartment style cabins, often have areas in restaurants reserved for them.

Choice

On most modern cruise ships, there are numerous speciality restaurants you can frequent. Obviously, the larger ships have more choice, but even smaller cruise ships have many restaurants to choose from – Italian, Japanese, Chinese, French and so forth. Some speciality restaurants even have Michelin starred chefs that pride themselves not only on the quality of their food, but on the number of courses they serve. It is not unusual to be served 20 courses in one sitting at some speciality restaurants, but they do have cardiac arrest equipment in the corner, and paramedics working as waiters – well perhaps not.

Finding Eating-Out Deals

If you spend more on the initial cruise, your options for free food may increase (this is very dependent upon the package you have purchased). For example, many suite apartments often have flexi dining included as standard, and may even have a number of visits to none inclusive restaurants included as part of the package. But even if you go for a standard cabin there are still deals to be had when aboard – but it might take a little digging, or research to find them. I am certainly not advocating you use the whole cruise to work out ways to get speciality food very cheap, or for free, but it might be worth a small investment of your time to find offers. A little research when relaxing in your cabin could make the difference between having a romantic evening together, and having to sit listening to some inane drivel from a passenger on your inclusive dining table wanting to explain his passion for collecting bottle tops (believe it or not, this has happened).

Many articles and blogs are written by people to help you get the cheapest and the best deals possible in speciality restaurants, and other paid for food and drink venues. These blogs/forums can certainly be very helpful, but unless you want to sit reading page after page of peoples' quirky suggestions, only to end up finding you have to eat at 2 am, and collect 1000 gift vouchers before the cruise, you might do well to follow this one simple rule. Turn your attention to the cruise newsletter, or leaflets left in your cabin. If you don't have any in your cabin, you should see them dotted about the ship. They are often full of offers and deals for places like the spas, as well as deals on speciality restaurants and eateries.

Generally, the offers are to encourage people to dine when it is a lean period for the restaurants, which is often at the beginning or the end of a cruise. At the beginning of a cruise, passengers are generally happy getting to know the ship, and their new dining partners at their inclusive dining table, so they often don't eat out. At the end of the cruise, passengers give the speciality restaurants a miss for a number of reasons, but it is generally because they want to say their goodbyes to new acquaintances they have made on their inclusive dining tables. Some also use the last cruise to thank their inclusive dining steward and give them a tip for the service they have provided.

Reserving a Table at a Speciality Restaurant

Many speciality restaurants will require you to book a table in advance, but you can just turn up on the night if they aren't busy. If you have booked a speciality restaurant and you don't turn up for whatever reason, you may be expected to pay for the meal or a percentage of it. As with tours, you can often cancel the meal 24 to 48 hours in advance if you change your mind. If you have any allergies or special requests, speciality restaurants can often accommodate you, although it is advisable to give them some advance notice as it is with your inclusive dining area.

Dressing for Dinner

Many restaurants that are open throughout the day often have no specific dress codes. Having said that, if you turn up with a swimsuit on, you might be asked to wear a little more. You may even see notices or pictures on the walls of some dining areas suggesting what not to wear.

During the evening, however, smart casual is acceptable, but on formal evenings, (which some cruises have at least twice on a 7-day cruise) you will be asked to wear a suit and tie. As mentioned previously, children are also required to wear the same formal attire for meals, and any functions they attend. Some cruise lines are more formal than others, and some cruise ships may require you to always wear formal attire for evening meals.

Ice cream, Pizzas, Cookies & Snacks

I mentioned in the previous chapter that some ice cream, pizzas and snacks are free – but you may also be expected to pay for them. Many passengers get caught out believing that the small eateries positioned on the lido deck next to the pool are free, when in fact many charge for this food. Generally speaking, if those serving you ask for your cabin card, or cabin number, a charge will be taken.

Don't get Caught Out

Make sure you keep track of how many treats you or your family consume on a cruise. Whilst little treats are fine, they can add up considerably if you don't watch out, unless money is no option of course, and then you might need to think about your waist-line.

Tips

1. Let the staff know if it is a special meal, (birthday, anniversary etc.) because they will often throw in a treat for you.
2. If you make a group booking in a speciality restaurant, they may even throw in extra wine for free.
3. Staying loyal to a speciality restaurant often means you will be given additional benefits, like free wine and soft drinks.
4. Deals for speciality restaurants can be found on leaflets left in your room, but don't become too obsessive about trying to find the ultimate deal, as it could ruin your cruise experience.
5. Even if a cruise line does not require formal attire, you may not be admitted into some dining areas unless you a dressed in smart casual clothing.
6. You are generally not required to dress for lunch, although you are usually asked to wear more than a swimming costume in restaurants.
7. If you book a speciality restaurant, you may be expected to pay for the meal, or a percentage of it if you don't turn up.
8. If you have food intolerances or special requirements, try to let the restaurant know in advance. Confirm that they have accommodated your dietary wishes before you eat your meal.

12

Drink

On cruise ships, you can buy buckets of beer, cartons of wine, and streams of soft drinks, but personally, I am waiting for baths of coke, swimming pools of spirits, and oceans of champagne before I go for the deal. You can even get alcohol for free, but it might only give you a very limited choice, or you may have to frequent parties and shipboard events to do so - meaning you will have to be very organised to avoid paying for alcohol completely on some ships.

Soft Drink

People often assume that since food is part of the all-inclusive deal, soft drinks will be the same, but often they are not. If soft drinks are included for free, it might be that only certain ones are part of a deal. You may also find you can only get soft drinks for free in specific locations, and at a certain time of day.

So how do you get around this? You could always take a 5 litre container to these venues and fill it every day with your favourite beverage. This would provide a constant supply in your cabin, but it would possibly have too much in common with camping. My advice is, if certain soft drinks are not included in the price of your cruise, decide how much you feel you will drink, and if it is a substantial amount, go for the constant refill offers you will often see advertised prior to the cruise, or whilst aboard (be aware that some special offers are only available at the time of booking).

If you aren't going to drink large volumes, just buy a soft drink when you want one, whilst occasionally being able to get one for free at select times and places. This is because the deals on sugary drinks may sound fantastic, such as 'JUST PAY $X FOR THE ENTIRE CRUISE FOR AS MUCH SOFT DRINK AS YOU AND YOUR WHOLE FAMILY CAN GUZZLE DOWN,' but on occasions you may need to drink the contents of the Amazon River to make this additional expense worthwhile. This is not to say there aren't great deals to be had on soft drinks, but parents may find if they go for these deals, they have constant sleepless nights chasing children around the cabin because of their vast sugar intake. In addition to this, with all the talk of diabetes, it would perhaps be prudent for most of us, whether we be children or adults, to reduce the number of sugary drinks we consume anyway. Unfortunately, when we have paid for something, the human tendency is to get our money's worth by having more than we would normally.

Water

The air-conditioned environment aboard the cruise ship and many tour-buses, together with the increased temperatures in some countries can cause you to dehydrate without you realising it. When on a cruise, it is important to drink fluids regularly. But before you reach for the bottled water in the fridge - STOP! It can often be that bottled water is not part of your inclusive cruise deal, and each bottle of water will probably cost you the national debt of a small country - or at least it can seem that way. Bottled water on many cruise ships is expensive, and the water from the taps is free, and is 'generally' good quality. I have highlighted the word generally because I would always suggest you check first, as this may not be the case with every cruise line.

Most of the water aboard cruise ships is either pumped from tankers ashore, or comes from desalination systems aboard, where water is extracted from the ocean through osmosis. This might make it taste a little different to what you are used to at home, but just add a touch of lemon and ice to it, which can be found in the buffet, and it makes the water taste great.

Coffee/Tea/Hot Chocolate

Being English, I love a cup of tea, and all flavours of tea including speciality teas are generally available for free on most cruises. Hot chocolate drinks are also generally free, although they may come in sachets (instant packets) of powder and milk mix. When I drink coffee I want it to be of good quality, and short of taking your own coffee machine aboard, buying a coffee is the only way to get a good cup on many cruise ships. You can certainly get gallons of coffee for free, but personally I don't think it tastes very good. There may be exceptions to this and I hope there are, but if there are, I never found them myself - but then I am a bit fussy when coffee is concerned. There are, however, bonuses to paying for a good cup of coffee because often you can get some excellent treats for free when you buy one, which you will not get anywhere else on the ship.

Alcohol

The laws for age consent when serving alcohol are different around the world, and it is important if you are between 18 to 21 that you know what these are if you want to drink alcohol. (UK 18 and the USA is 21 for example.) If you do not look your age, you will be asked to provide your ship card, or provide ID if you want to purchase alcohol on the ship.

Bringing Alcohol Onboard

Many passengers do try to bring alcohol aboard with them, either as they embark, or after they have visited a port. Different cruise companies have specific guidelines for passengers to follow in this regard, so it worth checking the cruise company's policy even if you have been able to take alcohol aboard other cruise ships before. Some cruise companies will allow you to bring a small quantity of alcohol aboard (a bottle of champagne or a bottle of wine) but many others will not allow any. Some cruise companies will store alcohol for you to collect when you leave, but check if it is OK to bring alcohol aboard before purchasing. It might result in your alcohol being left at the port, which may perhaps just mean that the local port authorities would have a slightly happier workforce that evening.

Free & Discounted Alcohol

If you have booked your cruise through the future cruise operator, you can often get them to throw in a bonus bottle of alcohol for when you join the ship. Many cruise organised functions, such as parties and events have free alcohol for all adult passengers. If you like the odd gamble at the casino, or go to art auctions and special events, often free alcohol is laid on to encourage a happy mood. Be careful in these situations though, because you may find you are so happy with all the free alcohol consumption, you come away having spent $20,000 on a painting, or having gambled your life savings.

Discounted alcohol is a similar story to soft drink, with many offers saying, drink as much as you want for $X. Whilst they may sound like good deals, many are not. There may, however, be some offers that are good deals but do your sums first, and decide how much alcohol you actually want to drink on the cruise. Even if you get a good deal you might be restricted to certain beverages, and the quality might be poor. You can often get extra measures by being loyal to a particular bar onboard, but you may have to tip a little more.

Over recent years there are certainly many more cruise lines that are offering soft drinks, and alcohol as part of their all inclusive deals. Even with these deals it is important to check what alcohol and soft drinks are included because it might be very limited. Sometimes your choices can be significantly increased by purchasing an upgrade offer either before, or whilst on a cruise.

Tips

1. Water is generally excellent drinking quality from the taps aboard cruise ships, (always check first) so save yourself some money by not purchasing bottled water all the time. Adding a touch of lemon and ice often makes tap water taste great, which can be found in the buffet.
2. Some cruise lines will not allow alcohol to be brought aboard their ships. In these situations, you can ask for it to be kept aboard for when you disembark. Be aware, however, they may not do this for you, but there is no harm in asking.
3. Free drinks can be had at many onboard parties. The champagne can be of a cheap standard and drinking too much might leave you with a bad head.
4. Taking an alcoholic drink to your cabin is acceptable with most cruise lines. Just remember to be mindful of other passengers if you are having a party, as walls between cabins are thin and do not especially stop sound.
5. Soft drinks can be included in an all-inclusive package deal, but I would check first, as some cruise companies do not include any free drinks apart from tap water.
6. Buy drinks in bulk if it makes financial sense.

13

Food – Weight-gain!!!

You will have to forgive me in this chapter because I do use it as an opportunity to have some fun occasionally, well how could I resist with such a subject before me. I have even had to *tone up* some of the jokes because they were getting a bit weighty.

With this in mind, you might want to take some of the things I say with a pinch of salt – perhaps not too much, as it is not great for your health. I would also like to make the point that I am not deriding any person of a larger size. I am just outlining things you might like to consider if you want your clothing to stay comfortable, or don't want to be purchasing additional garments regularly throughout the cruise.

Start as You Mean to Go On

On arriving at a cruise ship you quickly find yourself snacking on nibbles provided whilst waiting for your luggage to arrive onboard. On entering your cabin, you are greeted with a platter you have ordered as a special treat full of deliriously, delectable, delights. You then walk on deck and feast on the seasoned, savoury, samples that are offered for the ships Sail-away Party. You take the elevator/lift down to your room before dressing for dinner. At dinner, you are greeted by a 4-course meal full of spicy steaks, followed with sweet, sticky pudding. Only to return to your cabin where you find yourself toasting your cruise with another glass of bubbly, and even more cakes – and so it continues for the next week or two.

It is perhaps no surprise that when many people first go on a cruise they leave much heavier than when they arrived. After my first 2-months of 6-month contract on cruise ships, I can honestly say I was hardly recognisable. Looking back over my early photographs of cruising, I looked like I had applied a mahogany wood stain to my skin, and my body had the appearance of an inflatable dinghy.

Comfort

To address your weight-gain aboard a cruise ship, you could always take elastic clothes, of which there are many. Elastic is a marvellous substance and gives clothing a comfortable feel, whilst expanding to fit the new you. Perhaps the only problem with elastic clothes is, they give you the feeling that you are not putting weight on, when in fact your body is expanding faster than a bladder at the Scottish Bagpipe Championships. I believe Lycra can expand 4 times its size before breaking, so it might be something else to consider, although it isn't always as flattering as one would like.

Perhaps think about taking sarongs, and loose fitting flowing garments that are not only comfy but allow for cool air to circulate around your body. They also have the advantage of discreetly hiding any little bulges that may have appeared throughout the cruise.

Treats & Snacks

Perhaps a more appropriate way to approach this subject is to look at preventative methods for weight gain whilst aboard. It would certainly stop you wearing more elastic than the total balls used in the last open golf championship. Think about restricting yourself to only eating at certain times. The problem often isn't the main meals, its generally the additional food and drink consumed in-between.

Whilst it is nice to have a treat, a treat is only a treat when you treat yourself to a treat occasionally. Although you might say, the cruise is a treat and treating myself to a treat whilst on a treat is a treat, so because it is not a regular treat I can treat myself as much as I like because it is only a treat and not a practice. Very true, however, it is surprising how quickly you can put weight on if you aren't careful, and you might have to treat yourself to fewer treats so that when you get home, anything other than celery and lettuce is classed as a treat for the next 10 years.

Be Active

Many people who have never been on a cruise before might find it a surprise to hear that going on a cruise need not be all rest and relaxation. If you book a cruise that has mostly port days and you choose tours where walking or energetic activities are involved, you may find that you are so busy you hardly have time to snack and eat to excess. There are excellent gyms onboard and exercise classes, (these can be costly to use on some cruise ships) but with a little cleaver thinking you could avoid these altogether unless you particularly want to use them of course. With the cruise ships being so large, you can avoid using lifts (elevators) and use the stairs, try walking around the large expanse of decks or even break out into a jog. I would probably refrain from lifting passengers up for toning your muscles because you might slip a disc in the process.

Reducing the Wrong Food Consumption

Eating a balanced diet whilst you are aboard will almost certainly help you to reduce the chances of weight gain. Reducing sugars and balancing carbohydrates and proteins so ketosis (the burning of fat by increasing metabolism) starts, is certainly something you could think about. This isn't as hard as it sounds because there are often ample protein products onboard at no extra cost. I once had a friend who looked forward to returning to the ship because he lost so much weight.

Drinking more water whilst consuming less soft drinks and alcohol helps to reduce your sugar intake, and also has the effect of making you feel fuller. Not adding extra salt and sugar to food whilst aboard can also be beneficial, and you generally find the food has plenty in it anyway.

Why Worry What You Eat and Drink?

You may say 'why worry about your waist-line when you are on a cruise, just enjoy yourself.' If that is your opinion, I fully understand, and have a great cruise, just remember to pack plenty elastic garments or be prepared to invest in a new wardrobe of clothes.

Personally I feel its often inevitable that you will put on a little weight whilst on a cruise, especially if you haven't cruised before. But if you are a little concerned about putting on too much weight, perhaps have a little plan of attack before you even start the cruise.

Tips

Here are some slightly eccentric suggestions for keeping your weight down on a cruise.

1. Become highly stressed before and throughout the cruise.
2. Never take an elevator/lift, and run every staircase you encounter.
3. See the onboard hypnotist, because they can do wonders for your cravings.
4. Reduce the size of your plate to the size of a bottle top. This would require you to taking repeated visits to the buffet.
5. Get Norovirus, this will be discussed in a later chapter.
6. Only eat once a day, although that might equate to eating consistently all day.
7. Never have elasticated clothing, this is especially important around the waist area.
8. Bring clothes that fit exactly, and make sure you have no money to buy additional clothing or elastic.
9. Become fitness obsessed because there are plenty of places to go on a cruise to feed your addiction.

14

Types of Cabins

Cabins are often referred to in different ways on cruise ships, such as suites, mini-suites, staterooms, classics, standards, balcony, ocean view, sea view, inner cabins, partial view cabins, deluxe, and solo cabins to mention just a few. The main difference between them is, you get complete luxury in a select few, natural light in others, fresh air in some, and an internal dark and sometimes stale room in the rest – a bit harsh perhaps, but certainly true on some of the older cruise ships.

Ultimately, the cabin you decide upon will determine the feel of the whole cruise, so choosing the one that suits your needs is essential. To assist you in your decision making over the next 2 chapters I am going to look at the different types of cabins, and their locations on the ship. On each cruise ship there will be variations in size and comfort in each category, and it is certainly worth finding this out before you make your final decision on what cabin to choose when it comes to particular companies. Every company also sets up their cabin category slightly differently, and there is no one size (description) fits all. Because of this, you may notice I use the word 'often' or 'generally', generally quite often in this chapter.

Suite Cabin

A suite is often (not exclusively) situated on the upper floors of a ship, and has multiple rooms such as a lounge, bedroom/bedrooms, dining area and bathroom. They can have access to a much larger balcony/balconies, which may lead to a private swimming pool on some cruise ships. The bathroom often has things like spa baths, hot tubs, and they are generally more luxurious in size and comfort. The bedrooms often have more space, larger beds, and roomier wardrobes. The lounge will often include sofas, a large television, dining table and even an entertaining space for visitors. Executive suite cabins could be upwards of 1500sq ft/140 sq meters on some cruise ships, which is actually larger than the square footage of some new houses, and some may even have two floors.

Many suites certainly are very plush inside, and the level of quality and space is reflected in their price. On each ship, the size and furnishings of suites can vary enormously, so study the brochures of individual cruise lines before booking. They can also come with subsidiary benefits such as your choice of dining times at your inclusive restaurant, (flexi dining) reserved front-row seats in the theatre, and access to a private VIP area in the terminal. You may have a personal valet/butler attached to your suite, who will address any laundry needs and other requirements you may have. All of these features mean, they are also generally the most expensive of all the cabins on cruise ships. Having said that, you can also book mini suits, which have many of the trappings of a standard suite but are smaller, and therefore much less expensive.

Balcony Cabins

Waking up in the morning after a restful night's sleep, you pull aside the curtains and venture out on the veranda to inhale fresh ocean air whilst relaxing on your lounge chair. Bathed in a warm morning glow of the sun, your dreams of a perfect romantic, and seduction filled holiday are made manifest.

That is the theory anyway, in reality you have a small room that is often barely large enough to contain your bed/beds depending on if it is a double or twin. (Some balcony cabins could be as little as 170 sq ft/16 sq meters, or a little larger than a small garden shed.) Because of their size, you hear every noise your partner makes in the bathroom because it is so close to your head. To get to the veranda you need to climb over your bed, and scale a tower of suitcases. When you eventually arrive on the veranda, you can't even sit down let alone relax on a sun lounger. This is because if you get the cheapest balcony cabin it might be so small that two people of a moderate size can just about stand on it.

Unfortunately, when you book a balcony it doesn't mean anything until you do your research, not even the fact you will get fresh air. This is because there are also internal balcony cabins facing into the atrium of the ship on some cruise lines. Before you book any cabin, carefully look at the size and design as well as the sleeping arrangements, because the whole cabin might be smaller than your bedroom at home, and even be a strange shape.

Despite many balcony cabins being small, cramped and noisy, some balcony cabins do have redeeming qualities. The ones facing the ocean are often bright and airy, and you can experience outside vistas in privacy. This is particularly good if you are in a beautiful area, as you can share a special moment with the one/ones you love in an intimate way. These cabins may have a tendency to be long and narrow, but this can be worth the sacrifice if having access to daylight, fresh air, and views is important to you.

It is also far easier to look out from your balcony and see whales, dolphins, or other sea life. Added to this, if you are visiting lots of places, a balcony cabin affords you the opportunity to relax in your cabin when you enter and exit ports – which can be the most amazing experience.

Inner & None Standard Shape Cabins

Inner cabins can give you more space for your money, and many passengers choose them specifically because of their space to price ratio. Some inside cabins are unusual shapes as they are fitted around the ship's superstructure, and if you don't mind pipes, stanchions and a few other quirky features, many inner cabins can be a very cheap option. They are often a little larger as well, so if you have a large family there are generally more places to store cases etc.

The main problems people seem to find with an inside cabin is their lack of natural light and ventilation. Many people also don't like the fact that they can't see the outside scenery. You can get around these issues to some extent by turning your TV to an appropriate channel, to reveal outside images of the ship, and opening your door to your cabin regularly (only do this when you are in the cabin of course). But no matter how you dress it up, looking at a TV screen is not the same as experiencing something for real. It is important to remember that if you do take an internal cabin you can still go on deck and you are not restricted to one side of the ship either.

Window Cabins & Restricted View Cabins

Window cabins are essentially like inner cabins, with a small opening or window letting in natural light. Having daylight coming into your cabin changes the feel of a cruise, and personally I would pay a few extra dollars for this feature. They are also often a little larger than balcony cabins although you cannot guarantee they will have fresh air. Restricted view cabins can be found around the ship, and if you don't mind some of the ship's superstructure obscuring your view, they can be a substantially cheaper option. Sometimes this obstruction is only minimal, and hardly impairs what you see.

Decisions

Before deciding on any cruise ship cabin, think carefully what you want out of the cruise. If it is just to get away with the family for a relaxing time, and you principally want to use the facilities board, then a larger inner cabin might be just the thing. If you have booked a romantic getaway, being in an internal cabin with no view or in a small narrow cabin might not provide the atmosphere you were hoping.

Tips

1. Natural light is something that can make your cruise feel entirely different.
2. Suite cabins are very different from ship to ship, and not all companies offer the same fringe benefits for booking a suite cabin, so it is worth making sure you are getting what you expect to get.
3. Mini suite cabins are becoming more popular, and they offer a certain level of comfort in a much smaller room – they may also have other fringe benefits to them.
4. Inner cabins are often a little larger than balcony cabins.
5. Check cabin sizes on the ships plan, which you should find on the cruise companies website. They should give you square meter/feet sizes for their cabins.
6. Limited view cabins might not be as limited in view as you may imagine. Read reviews from other passengers who have been on that ship. You can also look at plans for the ship online.
7. Make sure you get the balcony type you want, and don't just expect balconies to be private, and face the ocean. This is because there are internal balcony cabins, virtual balcony cabins, shared balcony cabins, and so forth.

15

Cabin Quality & Locations

Some cruise lines will often only allow you to pick a category of cabin you want, and they will assign you a specific cabin. But there are some cruise lines that will allow you to pick the exact cabin you want when booking your cruise.

Cabin Category

So what exactly is a cabin category? It is simply a level of quality the cruise company ascribes to each cabin on the ship. For instance, you might decide to book an internal cabin, but there may be many more price options available for you within that category (which you could call sub-categories). These sub-categories are often determined by the size of the cabin, the position it is on the ship, and the quality of furnishings inside.

Don't make the mistake of believing that going for a higher category (priced) cabin will mean it will be better suited to your needs. You might find a larger internal cabin is cheaper than a smaller internal cabin because of their positioning on the ship, and the inside design of each. The larger cabin might be positioned close to a laundry or somewhere noisy, making it a cheaper option than the smaller one for example. It is this aspect of cabins that I will be discussing for the next few pages.

Noisy Cabins

I have a friend who has fallen asleep riding a bicycle, standing up in a rock concert, brushing his teeth, and playing tennis. However, most of us do not have his constitution and are quite sensitive to vibrations and sounds whilst sleeping. If you are keen to avoid a noisy cabin, look at the plan of the ship you will be sailing on. You can often view the plan online, or some cruise brochures have them inside, and they are generally quite detailed.

When looking at the ships plan, if you are keen to avoid noise, have a few things in your mind such as, is the cabin near where the anchors drop? Is it in a thoroughfare where the stamping of feet on stairs will be constant? Is machinery such as lift/elevator working constantly near the cabin? Is it positioned below the top deck where chairs are being constantly dragged across the floor transferring the noise through the ceiling of your cabin? Is it in the vicinity where there might be music, dancing, theatres, and other similar places? Is it close to an engine room, or places where there is a possibility of sound from machinery? Is it positioned close to laundry rooms, (both general and passenger) where large machines will be working night and day washing, and drying thousands of garments? Does it back on to a restaurant or kitchen, which are often active all night preparing for the following day?

Reading reviews from others on websites, in group forums, and social media can also assist you when making specific choices. But don't get too bogged down with them, as you can end up chasing your tail with the conflicting comments people make.

Quiet Cabins & Dealing with Noise

Having read the last couple of paragraphs, you could be forgiven for thinking that every cabin on a cruise ship has issues with noise and vibrations. You may be surprised to hear then, that there are actually many cabins on a ship that are perfectly quiet (the majority in fact). Generally speaking, if you avoid cabins at the top of the ship and others near the bottom, then you should get a quiet cabin. You may also want to think about choosing an internal cabin that is positioned in-between other cabins. Internal cabins are often much quieter than balcony cabins because there is less noise from the outside elements.

Despite finding a cabin in a quite location it might be that you have a disrupted nights sleep because a noisy neighbour. (It is advisable to move your bed slightly away from the metal walls if possible, as it can be noisy for other neighbours.) It may be that a party going on outside your cabin, or people are talking loudly outside in the corridor well into the night. Many cruise ships do not have a designated quite time, and they expect passengers to be respectful of others, which isn't always the case. Whilst it can be tempting to confront these situations yourself, you probably won't be in the best mood if you have had a disturbed nights sleep, and it might end up with tempers flaring. The simplest approach is to contact the pursers' desk and they will send security to discreetly ask people to move, or be quiet.

What Location on the Ship Should You Choose?

We have spoken about location in regards avoiding noisy cabins, but there is more to your cabin location than just avoiding noise. Many modern cruise ships are incredibly large these days, and it is no exaggeration to say that it may take upwards of quarter of an hour to get from one place to another. If you have a specific area on the ship that you like to frequent, being a 10 or 15-minute journey from it can make for an irritating cruise. If you are a parent, you will probably find that you want to spend a lot of time with the children by the pool, or in the youth area. For you, being close to the activities that will feature most prominently throughout the cruise is perhaps more important than anything else. If the cabin does happen to have noises from deckchairs throughout the day, it might be a small price to pay for the convenience of being close to specific areas.

It might also be important for you to be near a particular part of the ship for wheelchair, or walking frame access. Or perhaps the Spa is the main attraction for all the treatments and facilities you will be using over the holiday. Do you like to smoke and need a balcony cabin? (Not all cruise companies allow smoking on private balconies including E-cigarettes, and you will need to check first. Do not throw cigarette butts over the side as this is an offence, and can have a devastating environmental impact on the ocean marine life.)

Perhaps you would like a particular side of the ship because the views will be better? There might be a large group of you, and you want to organise cabins together on the same floor and area of the ship. You could even require 2 interconnected rooms close to elevators/lifts for older family members that need assistance.

Suffice to say there isn't one location that is best, all have their positives and negatives, but knowing what you want, helps you decide where you cabin is best positioned.

Free Cabin Upgrades

I have read articles and heard people suggesting different ways you can get cabin upgrades for free. Some suggest complaining about the cabin you have been assigned when you first arrive aboard. Others say, booking on less popular cruises is one sure fire way of being upgraded. Some people even suggest telling your travel agent you will only book through them, if they can promise a cabin upgrade. In my view, this is all a bit hit and miss, and it certainly wouldn't be putting you in a good mood if you don't get what you expect from the agent, or when you arrive aboard. One sure-fire way of getting free cabin upgrades is to cruise regularly with the same company, and if they have a reward scheme, you can often use it for a cabin upgrades.

Tips

1. Cabin upgrades on some cruises are possible if the ship is not filled to capacity, but don't count on them. Booking with the same cruise company regularly, having a cruise credit card, and special loyalty programs can help in getting upgrades.
2. Metal walls are a feature in most cabins, and any tapping or banging on walls means that sound can reverberate through to other cabins. If this is happening from a neighbouring cabin, ask your room steward to deal with it, as he/she can organise to move beds, and other offending things away from walls.
3. Confronting noisy neighbours might not always be prudent, and mentioning the situation at the pursers' desk would be more appropriate. Onboard security can enforce things if necessary, but generally it is done in a tactful and discrete way.
4. Noisy areas to be aware of include engine rooms, laundries, anchor areas, busy thoroughfares, theatres, restaurants, lift/elevators, and dance rooms to name but a few.
5. Cabin location can be as important as the cabin itself, and if you have a family, disabilities or a desire to be somewhere on a regular basis, choose a cabin that suits your needs. Cruise ships can be incredibly large, and it can be a long walk to get to places.

16

Cabin - Extras

As you are going to be on the ship for a week or two in most cases, it is worth making your cabin and sleeping arrangements as homely, comfy, and tidy as possible. You certainly don't need to bring your own rugs and throws for the floor, and a full complement of family photographs, which I have seen in some cabins on world cruises. I fully understand those passengers were going to be away for 4 months at a time. However, I am sure you wouldn't want to have a disrupted nights' sleep, or neck, and back problems from an uncomfortable bed or pillow. You certainly wouldn't appreciate broken bones or a serious injury because of falling over something in the darkness, and all because an item was not stowed away correctly. This is especially the case if you have children with you as space can be a premium in many cabins.

Sleeping

Everything can be plush and lovely in a cabin, but if you have a mattress that is too soft, hard, small, narrow, or uncomfortable, then your sleep may be affected – which ultimately ruins any cruise. It isn't always the case that the more you pay for a cabin the better the quality the mattress will be. If you do find that your sleep is compromised because of a mattress, ask for a replacement, explaining what the problem is. Very often stocks of a few mattresses (firm, medium, soft) are carried on most cruise ships.

Duvets and pillows on cruise ships might consist of feathers, and if you have allergies you can often ask for a replacement. Most cruise companies will carry both synthetic, and natural fibre duvets to address this issue. If you have a specific pillow for a neck or a back complaint, think about taking it with you.

Magnets

As most of you will realise from my earlier comments, the walls, doors and even some fitting of your cabin will most likely be made of metal. You can buy magnets that are essentially a hook and allow you to hang additional clothes, towels, caps, and a host of other things on them. Flat magnets are useful for putting your pictures, postcards or other ephemera, such as menus and special offers on the walls. Things are less likely to get lost if you use a magnet, and you can be easily reminded of important things without having to resort to looking through a pile of papers. (It is like having one giant fridge to hang things on.) Using a magnet/magnets on the inside of the toilet door to hold unattractive but important documents allows you to peruse their contents without them being a feature in the main cabin.

You can either bring magnets with you from home or buy them whilst you are away. I personally always take a few hook magnets with me, and only if needed buy the rest whilst away. If I do buy magnets whilst away, I tend to buy the ones that remind me of the places I am visiting. I have so many magnets now, apart from pulling out my fillings whenever I walk past the fridge they are the best memories I have of my cruising career. Caution is needed, however, because despite their size, magnets are quite heavy when in numbers, and you might end up paying excess baggage allowance for them if you aren't careful (which I have done).

Coat Hangers

As mentioned, space in all but some suite cabins, and a few others, is often at a premium on a cruise, and seems to be getting smaller with every new ship. Generally, the wardrobes in most cabins are only large enough to fit a few clothes, but if you do happen to get a slightly larger wardrobe in your cabin, often coat hangers are few in number or none existent. Wire coat hangers are a fantastic item to take with you in your luggage, because they don't weigh much, and take up almost no space. Cardboard coat hangers are also another option. If you forget to bring coat hangers, you can ask your steward if he/she has some you can borrow. They often have a few available because many passengers leave them behind.

Torch

Always have at least 1 torch with you in your cabin, and have it accessible and near to your bed. (Most mobile phones have a very good torch.) This is because it can be very dark in cabins, (especially internal cabins with no natural light) and if a bulb blows, you might not be able to see a thing. I have had a bulb blow at the end of my bed, and ended up breaking my little toe by tripping on my shoes; which should have been hung up - the pain was excruciating.

Accessible Storage

The crew often take shoe racks (the foldable materials kind) with them, because they are very lightweight and take up little space in their luggage. They essentially act as storage spaces to hold small belongings in one place, which might even include shoes. You can often hang them on the backs of doors, on the sides of wardrobes, and they are especially advantageous if you have children to hold all their belongings.

Electronic Reading Device

You are perhaps ahead of me at this point and my apologies for stating the obvious, but having all your favourite books on an electronic reading device is a great option. (Obviously, my guidebook can be exempt from this discussion if bought in paper form, as it is even more essential than a lifejacket.) If you desire to read a physical book, many cruise ships have good libraries onboard, and there are often hundreds if not thousands of books to choose from.

Additional Items

It might be worth taking some additional items with you to assist with your enjoyment of the cruise, such as walky-talkies for contacting each other aboard, instead of using mobiles. Take a small packet of balloons and ribbons for identifying your cabin because cabins on large ships can look very similar to each other. Pack non-scented bathroom/laundry products if you have allergies. Take a couple of small locks for any bags that you may need to place valuables inside. Pack a bottle opener and corkscrew for any drinks that are not opened in a restaurant, and take a small bottle that you can use to fill up with drinking water from the taps on the ship. Take a net bag to carry your washing to and from the laundry.

You might be thinking at this point that because you are only going to be on the cruise for a week, or 10 days, the suggestions outlined above are a little excessive, and a touch overkill. But it is surprising what a difference a few simple things can make to even the shortest cruise, and it can often make for a much more enjoyable and rewarding vacation. Having said that, if I were you, I would probably refrain from packing the kitchen sink because they might have a problem plumbing it in.

Tips

1. Having allergies may mean you need to bring a particular shampoo or soap with you. Often getting specific things you require is not that easy on cruise ships, or in many of the holiday ports the ship visits.
2. Dividers are often present in cabins to provide privacy for parents and children occupying the same room. If you don't have any in your cabin, ask your room steward if one is available.
3. Be mindful of what you throw down the toilet, because generally, they will only accept toilet paper and human waste. The outlet is often so small it gets blocked easily and it might take some time to fix, which would mean a smelly cabin and no toilet for some time.
4. Adapters/power strips are sometimes sold on cruise ships, but often they are quite expensive, so pop one in your bag before you leave. If you bring a power strip you need to make sure it is fine to use in your cabin. It may need a PAT test by the ships electrical team to make sure it is suitable. You can sometimes rent one aboard also.
5. If you are part of a group, take some walky-talkies, because it makes it easier to contact each other, and it could prove easier, and cheaper than using mobile phones.
6. Magnetic chalkboards are great for messages.
7. An alarm clock stops you missing tours.
8. Ear plugs can help you sleep in noisy places.

17

Cabin Card (ID Card)

When you carry your cabin card (Cabin Key, Identity Card, Cruise Card, or ID) with you, you are more than likely carrying the following information on them, or at least a variation of it: the name of cruise company, name of ship you are on, the cabin you are in, the date you arrived onboard, your personal details, your dining assignment, what muster station you are assigned to, and a few other things, some of which I will come to in the next chapter. This information is not visible externally on your card for security reasons, and companies differ with the information they place on cabin cards.

Getting Your Cabin Card

Once you have past through the security officials at the entrance to the port, you can now go through the process of boarding the ship. Prior to the cruise, you should have been sent your specific time window for embarkation of the cruise ship (which is often over several hours). Midday is generally when most of these boarding windows overlap, and it could mean a delay waiting as large queues of people try to board. If you arrive outside of your allotted time window, you may not be allowed access to the ship for some time.

In the terminal, an official will verify all your customs paperwork, passports, visas, (should they be needed) and any other documentation before you go through the X-ray machine (this is generally not as invasive as the airport X-rays). Any visas should be organised in advance, and if you have booked through an agent all of this should have been addressed at the time of booking. As you go up the gangplank for the first time to board the ship, you will be asked by a security official from the cruise company to look directly into a camera positioned inside it. The machine will record your image, and identify you as the individual associated with your cabin card (it can be slightly different to this on some ships).

Your image may or may not be present on your cabin card. (It is not common for a picture to be displayed on a cabin card these days for security reasons, but your image will show on the screen at the kiosk whenever your card is inserted.) Having the appropriate paperwork and documentation for children is also essential when boarding a cruise ship.

After going through ship security you are then given your cabin card/cards, and other relevant information by a cruise representative. This will include what cabin you are assigned to, any itinerary changes that may have happened, your dining assignments, and any other relevant information pertinent to the cruise. (Some cruise lines give out wristbands instead of cabin cards at this point, and passengers can collect their cabin cards on the ship – all in a desire to streamline the boarding procedure.)

On or Off a Ship

Identifying if a passenger is on or off the ship is perhaps the most important aspect of a cabin card. All passengers and crew for that matter, are required to slot their cabin card into the kiosk, (the same or similar kiosk that was used when they initially came aboard) and it registers whether they are exiting or entering the ship. Failure to register your card in the machine can give a false impression of where you are, which could even mean the ship leaves the port thinking you are aboard.

Despite vigilance from the security department to make sure every passenger and crewmember inserts their cabin card into the kiosk when entering and leaving the ship, they miss the occasional person at times. It is good to make sure that you register yourself on or off the ship so that security is aware of where you are.

I once heard of a woman that failed to inform the ship's security that her husband was not aboard when it registered that he was, and the ship sailed without him. When it was found out what had happened, she apparently said she wanted a relaxing cruise, and realised she wasn't going to get one with him aboard. I don't know what her husband thought of being left stranded in Ecuador, but forgetting to insert his cabin card into the machine gave his wife a good excuse to leave him behind.

Using Your Cabin Card Ashore

Whilst your cabin card does have all the information required whilst aboard, it is often not always sufficient for identity at customs. If you are from the USA, however, you can apply for a passport card, (similar in size to your cabin card, or credit card) which is not currently allowed for air travel, but it can be used on some cruise ships instead of a standard passport.

Damaging Your Cabin Card

There are times when your cabin card fails to open your cabin door. This is because it can get damaged easily by having bar codes rubbed off, its magnetism removed, becoming split, bent, or any number of things. If you should lose your cabin card, inform the purser's desk as soon as you are aware of it, and they will stop it from being used. If you should find a cabin card on or off the ship, return it to the pursers' desk (which often acts a lost and found department on many ships) and explain where it was found.

To prevent you losing your cabin card the pursers' desk is also more than happy to punch a hole in it so you can attach a lanyard (which you can buy aboard if you forget to bring one). The only problem I have found with doing this is, most cruise cabin cards are made of thin plastic, and punching a hole makes them rather flimsy. If you bend it slightly, the weakest spot seems to be the part between the punched hole and the edge. Very quickly a crack appears above the hole, and the card falls off without you knowing. Having lost a number of cabin cards this way, I decided to invest in a lanyard with a small plastic pouch you can slot the card into. They have served me well over the years and I haven't lost a cabin card since, although I have accidentally left it in my cabin. If this should happen to you, you can call the pursers' desk and they will inform security to open it for you. If you damage you cabin card or it stops working, you should also be able to get another card free from the pursers' desk.

Security

When purchasing most things onboard the ship you will generally be asked for your cabin card to complete the transaction (this will be discussed in more detail in the next chapter). Whilst this is certainly safer and more convenient than using credit cards in many respects, it is also important to keep your cabin card safe (don't leave it on tables or bars where you might forget it). Let's face it, you don't want to risk someone else using it at your expense. If you do happen to lose it, notify the pursers desk as soon as possible and they will cancel it, and issue you with another.

This brings me onto my final point; don't write your cabin number on your cabin card to remind you of what cabin you are in, which I have seen done a number of times. Sadly, as with any other area of life, cruise ships do have people aboard who will stop at nothing to get something for free at the expense of others.

Tips

1. Have your cabin card to hand when boarding a ship, as you can hold up the queue of people trying to get aboard whilst you are trying to find it.
2. Children require passports and papers when they go ashore, and many over a certain age are also issued with a cabin card on some cruise ships.
3. Try not to damage your card by placing it in tight pockets, as it can make it difficult to enter the ship, and it could mean waiting in queues to get a replacement.
4. If you are locked out of your cabin you can phone the purser's desk, and a security official will let you in with a master key.
5. You can request another cabin key if you lose or damage your original, and you generally don't have to pay for a replacement.
6. Insert your cabin card into the embarking/disembarking kiosk so that the security department is aware of where you are.
7. You may find your cabin card will split and fall off having had a hole punched in it, as they are often not very thick or strong. A better alternative as far as I am concerned is to buy a lanyard with a specific pouch attached to hold it in.

18

Cabin Card & Money

For your cabin card to take the place of your credit/debit card, a credit/debit card of your choosing is linked to your cruise account when you arrive aboard, or sometime prior to this. From that point onward any purchases you make aboard, and any deductions for gratuity will be through your onboard account, and cabin card. Whilst aboard you simply present your cabin card (or sometimes you give your cabin number) and voila, money will be removed from your account faster than you can say - 'would you mind if I checked my account to make sure I have enough money to cover this purchase?' Or perhaps slightly quicker actually.

It is perhaps no surprise to hear that when some passengers eventually get their bill on the penultimate day of the cruise they get a shock at how much money they have actually spent. Many passengers form long lines at the pursers' desk to make sure that there hasn't been a mistake made, but they soon realize the extra spending is because they have been a little over zealous buying treats.

But it need not be like this.

You can check your onboard account to make sure your spending is not getting too extravagant as often as you want. This can be done very easily on many ships by simply logging into your cabin TV, and checking your onboard account (instructions on how to do this will be provided in your cabin). If you should happen to find any anomalies in the charges to your account, you can address them whilst they are fresh in your mind. Being proactive in checking your account can also help you avoid standing with lots of other passengers who are all trying to sort out their bills at the pursers' desk on the penultimate, or final day of your cruise.

If you are on a ship where you can not check your bank account through your cabin TV, I would suggest you ask the pursers' desk to print off a copy of your account regularly throughout the cruise. This allows you to keep track of how much you are spending.

Getting Cash

Despite the fact that your cabin card acts as your personal bank/credit card whilst aboard, you may still need cash when on a cruise. This could be for cash purchases ashore, paying for taxis, tipping, and so forth. You can bring some cash with you of course, (there are limits to how much cash you can bring into some countries, but is usually when you get above a few thousand dollars) or you can withdraw it from ATM machines when you get aboard a cruise ship. Drawing money from an ATM aboard can prove a costly exercise as a fee can be charged every time you withdraw money from one. There might also be a limit to how much cash you can withdraw at any given time, and you can be charged by the ship, your bank, or both for this service.

You can get a cash advance in the casino or pursers' desk, but once again there might be a charge applied. The other alternative is to draw cash out from an ATM or a bank when you are ashore, which may work out a cheaper option, depending on which bank you are with. If you are going to do this, many ATM's will usually only dispense the currency of the country you are in, and it might not be the currency used on the ship. If you draw out a foreign currency ashore and then exchange it for another currency onboard you will generally be losing a substantial amount in the exchange process, as the exchange rate on cruise ships is often not the most competitive. If on the other hand you go into a bank rather than using an ATM to draw out your money, you can often get a currency of your choice or the one used on the cruise ship.

It is also worth mentioning, if you are going to pay for something on a credit card, always opt to pay it in the local currency, and not in your own currency $ or £ for instance. Let your bank decide the official exchange rate and not the person selling you the item, because invariably your bank will give you a better exchange rate than the vendor.

Take 2 Credit/Debit Cards

Just to keep things simple it is a good idea to take at least 2 credit/debit cards with you on a cruise. Use one credit/debit card exclusively for your cruise account and don't use it for other purchases. Also have a limit on the card that you do not want to go above. Keep the other cards separate to your account for all other purchases you may make. By keeping your bills separate it is much easier to keep track of what you are spending. It also reduces any risk of you going over your credit card limit by accident, and being charged overdrawn fees by your bank.

Free Extras/Bonus Money

If I was to think of one expression to keep in mind when it comes to cruising, (even life for that matter) it would be.

IF YOU DON'T ASK YOU DON'T GET.

Sometimes just by asking for freebie's when you book a cruise you can acquire little additional benefits, which you wouldn't otherwise have received. This is because those selling the cruise may not always be forthcoming with all the extras they can provide to entice you. Things such as credits towards meals, spa treatments, cabin upgrades, excursion deals, money towards alcohol and such like. Let me be clear though - I am not saying that every time you book a cruise, one, or all of these will be available to you, but asking for them just opens the possibility of you getting something that would otherwise not be offered.

You can also acquire bonus money/credit from cruise companies, which can be used for onboard products and services. This can come from purchasing another cruise whilst you are on a cruise, being a loyal customer to one cruise company, having a cruise company credit card, referring someone for a cruise who has not sailed with that company before, and the list goes on. A little research can often reveal numerous ways you can increase your potential for free upgrades. Sometimes having little additional credits can make a remarkable difference to a cruise.

There are many more options to help you get that little extra on a cruise, but I am sure you get the picture.

Tips

1. Exchanging money into small notes is excellent for giving tips, and can generally be done at the pursers' desk, and often with no additional charges applied.
2. It is important to make sure before you go on a cruise that you inform your bank that you are going away, and may need to draw money off your card in a few different countries.
3. US dollars are accepted around the world including many none US cruise ships.
4. The exchange rates on cruise lines are often not as good as what you will get if you exchange your money at home, or in a bank onshore.
5. Cabin safes are very common on modern cruise ships, but just remember to take your valuables out before you leave.
6. Accessing your onboard account can generally be done through your cabin TV, and looking at the literature in your cabin will provide information on how this can be done.
7. Bonus money can be gained in many ways, but if you are loyal to a particular cruise company they often provide freebies to keep you coming back.
8. Always pay for things in the local money when you use a debit or a credit card because the exchange rate will almost always be better than what a vendor is giving.

19

None Mainstream - Single Cruising

Until recently the majority of cruise companies have focused much of their attention on mainstream passengers, such as couples and families. Other 'none mainstream' passengers like those with disabilities, and people travelling alone were given little thought. Single (solo) cruisers were expected to pay a supplement to occupy a double or a twin cabin, and those passengers with disabilities had to work around any problems they faced as regards to access in none purpose-built cabins.

In the next 2 chapters I will highlight a few things you could consider to help reduce the cost of a cruise and improve your experience, if you fall into the none-mainstream category that is.

Single/Solo Cabins

Some cruise companies have pioneered single cruising for many years, but on the whole single cruising is something many cruise companies gave little thought to in years gone by. But there are changes in the air since the teenies started in 2010/11 – or should that be in-betweenies, I am not sure? Anyway, new cruise ships are being designed with single people in mind these days, as the number of Single Cabins (Studio Cabins) being included on many new ships is increasing to some extent. If you can get a single cabin when you book a cruise it can be cheaper than paying a single persons supplement on a double or twin cabin, but don't expect it to be half the price. I use the expression 'if you can get a single cabin' because despite the trend for single cabins growing, there still aren't many cruise ships that have large quantities of them. This means your choice of cruise ships, and ultimately destinations are reduced dramatically if you only want to book a single cabin.

The single cabins on many of the new cruise ships are certainly well designed, but they are often small and compact with a bed to match. Other cruise ships are converting doubles into 2 singles, but I can imagine space will still be a premium.

Shared Occupancy Cabin

Some cruise companies make solo cruising cheaper by offering twin occupancy cabins. This is when you book as a single person and the cruise company finds someone of the same gender to share the cabin with you. By doing this you should expect to pay much closer to a half fare for the cabin. If the cruise company can't find anyone of the same gender to share the cabin, the passenger will generally have the twin cabin for themselves at the same fare.

Whilst this is certainly worth thinking about, it should be considered carefully before doing. Perhaps ask yourself questions like: am I happy to share a cabin with someone I don't know, will I be able to cope with someone who may snore, will I enjoy a cruise in a cabin where someone is untidy, can I sleep with the sound from a television if they have trouble sleeping, and so forth? If you don't feel comfortable with answering yes to any, or all of these questions, it might actually be worth spending extra on a twin cabin supplement if a single is not available.

If you pay a supplement for a twin cabin, be aware of what you are being charged for. Whilst you can't expect it to be half price you shouldn't be paying double for a single occupancy twin room. In fact, it is possible to pay less for a double/twin than it is for a single/solo cabin on occasions. This is because cruise companies sometimes reduce the price of doubles and twins to fill them up. So always check the prices of double/twin cabins, and don't always assume that a single/solo cabin will be cheaper.

It is also important to pay careful attention to any additional charges that may be levied on a double or a twin cabin. Some cruise lines might charge you less for the twin room, but charge you the full (double) price for things like – taxes and port charges. You may also find you get an inferior quality cabin in a less than desirable location if you pay a double/twin supplement.

Travel Agents

Travel agents are certainly good to use if you want all the stress and worry taken out of booking a cruise, but they can also be a real benefit for the single cruiser. They often provide opportunities for the single cruiser to meet more single people aboard. They do this by organising specific cruises for singles to go on, and provide activities aboard to help single people interact with each other. They can offer singles group coffee evenings, singles excursions, singles parties, singles dances, and so forth. Surprisingly the prices of these specialised cruises can be very competitive, and they can work out cheaper than if you were to organise your own cruise.

Group Bookings

Joining singles groups on social media that are organising their own cruise is another option you might consider. The savings can also be very good if the group has a substantial number going, as they can negotiate a better deal with cruise companies. There are, however, a few things to keep in mind with these arrangements. If you join a group, it may have tours and excursions booked as part of the deal, meaning you can not choose the tours you want. You may also have to share a cabin with someone, which means you will be spending a considerable amount of time with someone you perhaps don't know, like, or have anything in common with apart from cruising. In many groups, you also tend to have the dominant person who has booked the whole adventure, and they have a lot to say about everything. Sometimes you can spend half of your time being bossed around to do things, which you would otherwise have avoided. Even if you know all the group beforehand just remember that people are often very different when on vacation.

Organised Activities

Many cruise companies are starting to understand there is a growing market in single cruising, and some are designing activities aboard for this group. These include single persons' discos, dances, games, tours, events and even special evening meals. If you are considering finding a partner, taking a cruise might be something you could consider.

Many cruise ships even employ what are often described as escorts for single people onboard. Perhaps I should explain this a little before you get the wrong idea! It has been a well-documented fact that many mature single ladies like to travel on cruises, and the cruise companies provide gentleman hosts for them to dance with, and generally entertain these ladies in a professional way.

Things are slowly starting to change in the cruising industry for single people. If things continue to progress, single people might even be considered as being mainstream by cruise companies – but then, it is probably a long way off.

Tips

1. Specialist travel agents can make your cruise bespoke, and can include activities onboard to help you to make friends and perhaps even find a partner.
2. Taking a friend with you can help to keep costs down, but make sure you are prepared to be flexible. Sometimes, it is better to pay extra than ruin a good friendship, or have an unhappy cruise.
3. Single cabins on new cruise ships are certainly well designed, but they are often small and compact with a bed to match. They are also not generally half the price of a double/twin cabin.
4. Specialist websites for single cruisers might require you to share a cabin with someone else.
5. You need to be 21 years of age to travel as a single person on some cruise ships, and over 18 on others.
6. More single cabins are starting to appear on cruise ships, but you may need to book well in advance because they are not in great numbers even on the newest and largest cruise ships.
7. Forums and social media are starting to play a key role for people getting together to form their own groups in taking cruises.
8. Your options of cruise companies and destinations can be reduced substantially if you only want to book a single cabin. Being prepared to try other options such as sharing can increase your choices of cruises.

20

None Mainstream – Cruising with Disabilities

What cruise company you decide to sail with will often determine what you can expect in regards to facilities aboard. The laws in the UK and Europe are clear in making sure a person with disabilities cannot be discriminated against or refused access onboard a ship/boat unless it is unsafe to do so. Having said that, some cruise companies don't have specific insurance to cover them for people with a certain level of disabilities, so they may occasionally refuse a booking.

Cruise companies are also required to assist passengers if notice is given (this is usually 24 or 48 hours). The law at the present time (according to my understanding) does not identify what percentage of cabins are required to have disabled facilities aboard, or what those facilities should include. Whilst American cruise ships, and foreign-flagged ships sailing in American waters are required to be registered with American Disabled Access, (ADA) there are no current standards that specifically identify cruise ships. This means there is a disparity in what each cruise company chooses to do on their ships in regards to disabled access, and facilities. Because of this, you would do well to check what access/facilities are available for your specific requirements on the ship you are thinking of sailing on.

Social Media/Travel Agents

There are forums and social media sites that have been specifically set up to assist you in your choice of cruise vacation. They discuss certain ships, look at cabin layouts, identify problem ports for wheelchair access, discuss access for visual impairment, signage for brail, hearing loops, and many other things that may be of interest to those with disabilities, or those assisting others.

There are also online travel agents that are keen to do all the work for you, similar to those agents for passengers traveling alone. They are often more specific in providing details in regards to cabin layouts, port access, onboard facilities, and what tours may work well for those with certain disabilities. As they have experience of providing for passengers with disabilities, they can make life that much easier, and reduce the amount of research required by you.

Mobility, Lifting and Hoisting Equipment

There are approved companies that can rent mobility, hoisting and lifting equipment to you, but you can certainly take your own if you so desire. Perhaps the advantage of renting the equipment is it can prove more convenient in the long run, especially if you are requiring something large. The cruise approved suppliers are specifically set up to work with port authorities, and thus are well positioned to provide for cruise passenger's in particular. They often take any equipment you have rented directly to the cruise terminal or on to the ship to get you acquainted with its features whilst removing it after the cruise. If you are unsure what companies to use, look to online forums or social media sites to see what others are recommending.

If you do take your own equipment you have to make sure it will fit in your cabin because mobility scooters, and other equipment cannot be left in corridors on many ships. It is also important to make sure that wheelchairs and mobility scooters can fit through all the entrances in your cabin, as bathroom doors can be narrow.

Tours

Getting to the shore to go on tours can be challenging for many with restricted movement. If the ship is mooring out at sea, getting wheelchairs onto the tender can be difficult if the weather is bad. Added to this, choosing an appropriate tour that will accommodate your needs is paramount. Unfortunately, I have seen passengers with disabilities book a tour and not be able to join it, as there was a problem with accessing the transport. This could include getting on to a specific boat or accessing a bus. If you are concerned about access onto transport ask the tour excursions department aboard for advice, and if required they will contact the tour company to find out more information for you. Tour companies will often do their utmost to accommodate passengers needs, but it is sometimes not possible to take mobility scooters on buses and small boats, but wheelchairs are often accepted.

Cabins for Disabled Access

Many new cruise ships have cabins specifically purpose-built from the ground up to accommodate passengers with certain disabilities. Other cruise ships have had cabins altered to accommodate the needs of these passengers. The difference between the two cabins can be poles apart, and in the purpose-built cabins, entrance to the rooms can often be wider, space inside the cabin may be larger, floors may be smoother, bathrooms easily accessible, and switches lower. Just because the cruise company says it is a cabin for disabled access, it doesn't mean it will accommodate your needs. Look at their website or brochures to find out exactly what the cabin layout will be.

Traveling with a Companion

I am sure most people with a disability highly value their independence as we all do, and many have fought tooth and nail to preserve it. When it comes to cruising there are some situations when having a companion with you is a distinct advantage, especially if you feel you may need assistance regularly whilst aboard. Whilst a companion may often not be required in normal life, and to do so takes away a certain level of independence, many cruise companies encourage people with specific needs to have a companion who can assist them.

Crewmembers are always willing to assist in many respects, but it can mean waiting for some time for a that help. Having a companion stops the need to wait around, and if there is specific machinery that is needed such as hoists for instance, your companion would be more adept to handle your personal needs than crewmembers.

Times, They Are Changing

I am fully aware there is more to this subject than what a single chapter can convey, but hopefully, it will give you something to work with. If you are thinking of taking a cruise, I would recommend you do your own thorough research, and look up any organisations that might assist.

Despite the fact that having a disability can mean a little more research than mainstream cruising, it certainly should not stop anyone from taking a cruise. It is also encouraging to see cruise companies are starting to seriously consider cruise passengers with disabilities, but there is still some way to go.

Tips

1. Consider taking someone with you if you think you will need assistance because you may have to wait around for crewmembers to assist you.
2. Accessibility in the rooms of non-purpose built cabins can still be a problem, and looking at ships plans and photographs can help a little. Often, it is a recommendation from others that is the most beneficial when it comes to taking a cruise.
3. On some older ships the buttons for elevators/lifts can be hard to reach if you are in a wheelchair.
4. Adequately charge mobility scooters before going ashore, or you could find yourself unable to get back to the ship, and always take the ships phone number with you when going ashore.
5. Ask for additional space around the table before dining at your inclusive restaurant, or when booking at a speciality restaurant.
6. Renting equipment from an organisation that deals regularly with cruise companies reduces the chances of any complications in delivery.
7. Social media is becoming the go-to place to look for advice and suggestions in cruising with disabilities. There are many sites which offer valuable information free of charge.
8. Specialist web companies are available to look after all of your requirements, and can cater for every aspect of your cruise.

21

Seasickness (Mal De Mer)

Mal de mer or seasickness as it is generally known is uncommon with passengers on cruise ships. This is not surprising when you think of the size of the modern cruise ships. Even large waves of 8-feet plus have little effect upon the movement of these leviathans, such is their height, weight, length and girth. Their length means that instead of going up and down waves they simply float over the top of the ocean, ironing out the overall feel of the journey. That is not to say they aren't affected by adverse weather conditions. Serious storms coming from hurricanes can create a very uncomfortable ride for those prone to seasickness.

When sailing in particularly bad weather many cruise ships have an unusual motion to them. This is probably due to their top heavy design which attracts the wind like a sail, and their relatively shallow drafts (which are specifically designed in such a way to allow them to get into more ports). The modern cruise ships reduce this rocking or yawing motion by extending stabilisers out of each side if the weather becomes unsettled. They increase the surface area on both port and starboard (left and right) sides of the ship, which helps to reduce the extremes of movement. This generally makes for a much more comfortable cruise even in rough weather. Unless you are very unlucky, or the weather is particularly bad, you shouldn't feel seasick on a cruise.

Why do People Feel Seasick?

It has been suggested by some researches that some cases of seasickness might actually be psychosomatic. In other words, seasickness may actually be induced because someone is worried they might be seasick, and the fear of what may happen induces it. It is even suggested that some people can actually feel slight aspects of seasickness even before for they set foot on a floating craft because of the fear of what may happen when they get aboard.

For the most part, however, seasickness or motion sickness happens because the brain's balance-sensing system can not come to terms with the movement that is going on around it. This is because it is accustomed to stable land, and when something different comes its way, (like a moving ship on the waves) it can struggle to adapt. That is why looking at the horizon can help to to lessen the feelings of nausea on a rocking boat/ship because the horizon provides a fixed reference point despite everything else moving around. Obviously, looking at the horizon is not a serious option on a cruise, as you are on the ship for days, not hours.

Some people are also more prone to seasickness than others - so what do you do if you are on a cruise and you suddenly start to feel seasick?

Be Busy

It may perhaps seem like a strange suggestion, especially when you are on a cruise to relax, but at the first onset of seasickness try to keep you brain active by doing something. It is thought that being active counteracts the feelings of nausea because it focuses your mind on doing something, which if nothing else reduces any thoughts you may have about being seasick.

Wristbands & Food

Wristbands are designed to place pressure on a particular point on your wrist. It is this specific point of pressure that seems to work for many passengers, and crew in stopping the effects of seasickness.

There are also many foods that can work very well for seasickness such as, ginger, green apples, and smelling orange peel. Eating little and often can also help, and some passengers and crew find just having a good meal is enough to make them feel much better in rough weather. With the abundance of food on cruise ships, eating certainly shouldn't be a problem.

Pill's & Patches

One very good way to reduce seasickness is to take pills or to use a patch. They work by blocking the information coming from the nerve signals to the brain. This stops the signals traveling from the brain to the stomach, which induces nausea. Whilst they can work remarkably well for many, their ability is short lived. It might require you taking them very often throughout a cruise if the weather is unstable, so take plenty with you whilst following the recommended dosage on the packet.

People can have allergic reactions to medication, so if you have never used a product before it is always a good idea to make sure you do not have an adverse reaction prior to using it. In addition to this, pills and patches often take a while to start working, and you might be on a rocking ship quite quickly after boarding, so take any medication well before the cruise if you are concerned you might need it. It is important to note, however, some seasickness medication can make you feel drowsy, so if you are going to take them prior to a cruise, be aware of what you will be doing (driving etc.) and make any necessary adjustments to your schedule.

The Onboard Medical Department

There are times when all the patches, being active, wearing wristbands, eating specific food, and not thinking about seasickness, will have no effect on you. On these occasions you need to call a doctor or go to the medical centre onboard. They will usually inject a substance into you which generally reduces or even stops the feeling of nausea. I have seen passengers who were feeling diabolical, completely recover in a short time having had the injection.

The cost of medication for seasickness is approached differently depending on what company you are cruising with. On many cruise lines seasickness pills are available for free from the medical department, but if you go to the shops onboard you can expect to pay. When it comes to getting an injection, this often requires a payment, and it can be rather expensive – but passengers who have had the injection generally say it was money well spent.

Choice of Cabin

The position of your cabin can make a surprising difference to the movement of the ship. Cabins that are low down, and in the centre of the ship have less movement, and can supposedly reduce the chances of you feeling seasick if the ship is moving around. Having said that, there is often no substitute for fresh air and seeing the horizon when you feel sickness coming on. But considering extreme weather conditions are rare on cruise ships, I wouldn't be planning your whole cruise based upon the positioning of a cabin to avoid seasickness – unless you a particularly worried about it I suppose.

Tips

1. Seasickness pills and patches are readily available in the shops and the medical centre onboard.
2. Allergic reactions to some seasickness medication does happen.
3. Visit the onboard medical centre to get free or very inexpensive seasickness pills during opening hours. The cruise company wants you to have a memorable holiday for the right reason, and because of this, many cruise companies don't charge for seasickness pills.
4. The seasickness jab can sometimes be free, and even if you have to pay, it is well worth having it as it acts fast, and can transform how you feel. Once again, be careful of any possible reactions you may have to it, and speak to your doctor before taking a cruise if you have any concerns.
5. Choosing an inside cabin in the middle of the ship reduces the movement, but fresh air and seeing the horizon from a cabin with a balcony can also help to counteract seasickness, so I suppose it is a case of weighing up your options
6. Children's seasickness pills and patches are available, but seek your doctor's/health professional's advice before using them. It is thought very young children up to 3 or 4 are not prone to seasickness.
7. Seasickness remedies include ginger, green apples, pressure bands and many other personal remedies.

22

Medical Centre, Insurance, Illness & Death

A cruise is supposed to be an opportunity to relax and escape stress and worries, but on rare occasions it can turn out to be the exact opposite. Unfortunately, passengers have accidents, illness occurs, or someone close to you dies whilst aboard. Being prepared if these things should happen is vitally important. This not only includes having the correct insurance to cover you for every eventuality, it also means taking appropriate steps before a cruise, and whilst aboard, to reduce any risks you may have.

Medical Centre

Most of the larger cruise ships have 2 doctors and a number of nurses aboard. The medical centre on cruise ships may either be run by the cruise line, or franchised out to an external company. Modern medical centres are often state of the art with all the medical equipment one would expect for a ship carrying thousands of passengers. They often have enough equipment for general ailments and some serious situations, but generally they do not include facilities and equipment for operations. This means if a serious accident or illness occurs that needs more specialised equipment, passengers are usually disembarked and taken to the nearest hospital.

If you do need to visit the medical centre whilst aboard you may have to pay for a consultation, even if you haven't received any treatment or medication. You will also probably be expected to pay for any visits to the medical centre whilst aboard. You should be able to claim this back from your insurance provider at a later date (depending upon your insurance cover of course.) The cost of visiting the medical centre can be prohibitive if you need serious medical treatment.

If you need the medical centre when it is not officially open there will always be a 24-hour emergency number to contact medical staff if required (you can get this at the Pursers desk). If you have a medical condition before you go on your cruise, make sure you take plenty of supplies with you should you require them. This is not to say that you won't be able to get them aboard, but as with anything, it can be very expensive. (Check before the cruise to see if you need to take any documentation for your medication.) Depending on your medical condition, it might also be a good idea to take medication with you when you go ashore. Some tours can be many miles away from the cruise ship, and running out of your medication in some places can cause complications. If for some reason you miss the ship you will also have a supply of medication with you. Just remember to take any documentation that may be required for them when you go ashore, as customs may need to see it.

Insurance

If you are on a cruise and you miss a substantial amount of the holiday through illness, there might be some recourse to claim a refund from your insurance company. If you are feeling unwell prior to taking a cruise, most insurance companies will cover you for cancelling if you get a medical certificate. Make sure you tell insurance companies of any medical history, as hiding it could make your insurance invalid.

Read any small print on your insurance policy thoroughly to be sure you are fully covered – and I stress the policy and not just the cover letter or email sent to you. You may be sent an email or a cover letter suggesting what you are covered for, but it is always important to read your actual policy thoroughly as their may be a disparity between the cover letter and the policy. The reasons for this are many, but insurance companies change their policies regularly, and it may be that the cover letter has not been updated. You should have a 14 day cooling off period, (this cooling off period may vary between countries) which means you can cancel your insurance in this time if it does not suit your needs. This cooling off period is to make sure the policy suits your requirements, which means you are expected to read it in full. It may be a little tedious to read but it is certainly worth the effort. I have spoken to many people who thought they were covered properly, but when it came to claiming from their insurance provider, they found out things were not as they initially thought.

When taking out insurance don't make price the deciding factor. It is too simplistic to think that a high priced insurance will cover you for everything, or a cheap insurance will mean you have limited cover. Insurance companies specialise in the cover they offer, and you might find a reasonably priced insurance, which covers you for cruising much better than one costing much more. Cruising has many aspects to it, and finding an insurance that covers you for every eventuality is essential. It might even be that you require a private jet to take you home should you get ill or have an accident. As previously discussed, if you are going to rent motorcycles, quad bikes, jet skies, or such like; or engage in extreme activities such as white water rafting, or extreme sports; make sure you are covered properly.

Illness & Vomiting

When you board a ship, you will generally be given a form where you can say if you, or anyone in your party have been sick recently. This simply helps the medical department monitor any signs of Norovirus, (winter vomiting bug, or SRSV) and perhaps any other illnesses throughout the cruise. Norovirus can take a few days after infection before any signs of it are evident. These symptoms include, projectile vomiting, and an upset stomach and diarrhoea for up to 3 days. Norovirus outbreaks are not a cruise phenomenon as some people seem to think, they are actually prevalent in any area where large amounts of people get together, such as offices, hotels, and large gatherings. We perhaps hear about Norovirus outbreaks more on cruise ships because of the need for sensationalism in some media organizations.

Norovirus is the cause for millions of gastro upsets around the world each year, and is even responsible for causing a substantial number of deaths in some developing countries. In western countries, however, the vast majority of people will make a full recovery in a few days.

Norovirus is highly contagious, and often contact with an infected person, or touching something that has been infected can lead to catching it. Thankfully most cruise lines don't have epidemics of it, and keep it to a manageable level if it is on a ship. Extreme vigilance from crew and passengers alike can keep the contamination to a minimum when an outbreak occurs on a ship. This vigilance includes, preventing passengers from serving themselves, condiments being removed from tables, everyone washing their hands regularly, and making use of the ample hand sanitizer that is distributed around the ship. If any person does show signs of the virus, they may be quarantined in their cabin for about 3 days. (If you are sharing a cabin with someone that has Norovirus you may be quarantined also.) Food will be brought to you regularly, but generally you will not be able to leave you cabin to explore the ship or any port until the doctor has given you the all-clear. You may be able to claim for the loss of days from your insurance provider depending on what insurance cover you have.

Death

Sadly, death does occur on cruise ships, and most ships have a morgue to place deceased people inside. It isn't a common practice to bury people at sea from a cruise ship, as documents' are required and stringent laws prohibit bodies from being dropped overboard in certain waters. Generally, when someone dies their body will be sent back to their home from the nearest port.

Tips

1. If you are unsure of what medication you can take ashore ask at the pursers' desk.
2. Quarantine for an illness such as Norovirus can be up to 3 days, but if your cabin partner/children get ill in the same cabin, it could mean an extended period being in quarantine.
3. Disruption of a cruise for virus outbreak will be evident by not being able to serve yourself at the buffet, more sanitation stations appearing around the ship, and condiments being removed from tables. Before you eat, board, and disembark, you will also be asked to sanitize your hands.
4. Eating uncooked food ashore particularly fruit, and vegetables can be dangerous, as they can be washed in contaminated water in some countries. Uncooked food on the cruise ship is fine to eat as hygiene is meticulous.
5. All liquids purchased ashore should have the tamper proof ring attached. This is because drinks can be made from local sources of polluted water (ditches, ponds and rivers). Many people selling them simply fill bottles with this water, and add a powder concentrate to it. Drinking from bottles without a tamper proof ring ashore, can make you seriously ill.
6. Visiting the medical centre aboard can be very costly. If you generally require specific medication, take it with you on a cruise because it could prove expensive sourcing it aboard.

23

Internet Services & Mobiles

Internet access seems to becoming increasingly more important in all of our lives as each year passes. Whether this is just a ploy of modern society to perpetuate the need for people to be consistently occupied in purchasing products to keep society afloat, is something I need to research on the internet one day.

It certainly seems to suggests that as we all become ever more dependent upon the internet, our vacations are becoming increasingly dictated by how good the service is. The only problem is, and it is a big problem, most cruise ships don't have internet that is fast enough and cheap enough to make this as easy and inexpensive as it is on land at the moment. (Obviously this section of the guide is more prone to be out of date, and things might have changed if you are reading this book in a few years, although that might be the case for the whole book.)

What Service to Expect

Some cruise ships are better equipped than others, and some companies are better equipped than others when it comes to the offering internet access on their ships. This is because some cruise companies have invested substantial sums into buying large amounts of bandwidth from telecommunications centres, or are teaming up with other companies to rent a satellite for themselves. They are also updating systems aboard ships so that internet access is ship wide, and not confined to a few select areas. Despite this, even on the most technologically advanced Wi-Fi ships, you will undoubtedly notice a difference in service to what you experience on land.

On a cruise ship you can still expect the internet to be slow and intermittent, depending on where you are in the world, and where the ship is positioned in regards to a satellite signal. This is because the internet signal on a ship needs to have an unobstructed path from it, to the satellite. If something obstructs that signal, like a mountain, a building, or a hill, that path will be compromised. So you could actually be moored next to the shore and not be able to access the ships internet, but if the ship is in the middle of the Pacific Ocean you could very well be able to get internet access without a problem. Cruising through Fjords for instance, can cause issues because the mountains surrounding the area impede the internet signal.

The Price of Cruise Internet

Despite some cruise companies providing internet package deals, these deals still couldn't be classed as inexpensive – although I suppose that depends how important you feel the internet is. Given this situation, what do you do if you want to contact home via the internet without having to stand on your head with one arm in the air, and pay a fortune to do so? You might want to follow the example of crewmembers because they can't afford to use the onboard internet for extended periods themselves. They do, however, want to have real time conversations with family and friends, check their bank accounts, and go on social media.

Crewmembers generally go online when the ship is at a port, as there is often a free Wi-Fi signal to be had off the ship. Many crewmembers take a small amount of time out of their working day to go to a local café or bar and benefit from fast internet access for the price of a cup of coffee or a beer. If you are unsure of where these places are, it is often best to ask a crewmember or go to a local travel information centre ashore. Failing that, just ask at the nearest bar and they will more than likely have customer Wi-Fi themselves. The port lecturer aboard is also an oracle of information in this regard, and can often point you to specific places ashore.

If crewmembers do need to use the onboard internet, they try to keep costs down by preparing what they want to send before even logging on. When they are logged on to the internet, they can simply attach a folder of images or cut and paste a prepared script from a document onto an email or something similar (apps are also available to help you do this). Crewmembers also choose the times when the internet is more likely to be less busy, such as the evenings, early mornings or when most of the passengers are ashore. Using social media, and sending emails without attachments is often generally quite efficient from the ships internet even during busy times - if there is a signal of course. This is because very little band width is used in social media, unlike when you send attachments of photos or videos. If you are going to send a photo attachment try to send it on a lower resolution and use an App (application) that is specifically designed to send images, as it can be a much cheaper option (you are generally given a choice of resolution sizes when you come to send it from a phone).

Mobile Phones

Perhaps it is not surprising that mobile phones are becoming indispensable in our lives when we think what they can do. They aren't just for making calls, checking emails, browsing the web, or playing games these days. Through App technology they can connect to devices in our homes, such as surveillance cameras, and heating systems. We can check that we have switched off all appliances, locked our homes, or have been burgled. But despite this, smartphones might be stealing cash from us in another way. This is because they may constantly be roaming for updates by connecting on to the internet, which can prove very expensive on a cruise, depending upon the network or plan the user has signed up to. There are a few ways you can stop this from happening, and switching your mobile phone to 'Aeroplane Mode' is perhaps the most fail safe way. But by doing this you are limited in what you can do with your phone. You could also turn off the mobile roaming feature on your phone by going into the settings function.

If it is particularly important for you to get the internet aboard, you can also get good deals from your service provider. If you sign up for the right plan it can mean you don't have to worry about roaming charges at all whilst you are away because they are included in you package. Alternatively, some people opt for inserting a separate

SIM-Card into their mobile, especially for use whilst they are away. These SIM-Cards are often pre-paid and calls from certain countries are very cheap. Sufficient to say, there are many options to reduce costs on mobiles these days, but being proactive before a cruise is usually your best bet. Failure to take the time to look at different mobile phone service options could mean you end up with a costly bill when you get home.

Emergency Contact Number

It is also worth remembering to leave all contact information with your family and friends back home so they can contact you in the case of an emergency. Don't just think it will be enough to leave your mobile number with someone back home, this is because your mobile might be out of service, or not be able to get a signal for a substantial amount of any cruise. All cruise ships can communicate with the shore at all times, so leave the contact details of what ship you are on, where you are going, and the company you are sailing with, with your family or friends before leaving for a cruise. It is also advisable to inform someone before you leave home of the day you are expecting to return.

Tips

1. The onboard internet will generally not be as fast as your superfast home broadband. Expect the internet to drop-out in some areas of the world, although the USA, Caribbean and Europe are much better.
2. Leaving the cruise companies/ships contact details with your family or friends before your cruise is still important despite carrying a mobile phone with you. This is because the service might be intermittent or none existent in some places, and in an emergency your family/friends can still contact you through the ship.
3. The onboard internet signal may be reduced or none existent even if you are close to the shore.
4. For mobile phones that aren't waterproof, take a waterproof cover as you may very well be near the pool, on a beach or a tender.
5. Use the calendar device on your phone, as it can remind you of any important times and events whilst aboard.
6. Alarm clocks & lights are available on nearly all modern mobile phones. This can save you carrying additional items that add weight to your luggage.
7. Use a lower resolution if you are going to send an image/photograph on your mobile. Larger images/photographs sometimes won't send from a cruise ship because of band width issues.

24

Cruise Photography & Video

Having professional photographs taken whilst on a cruise is still very popular, but perhaps not as much as it used to be. Many passengers conclude that there is no point in having their picture taken professionally because it costs money, when they can take as many selfies and pictures as they want with their mobile phone. Whilst this is certainly true, there is still something to be said for purchasing at least some of the professional cruise photographs that are taken of you, and your party throughout a cruise.

Many of the photographs we take digitally may get lost through corrupt computers, hard drives failing, and phones/cameras/memory cards being lost. Preserving this special vacation in print means, those images will be with you for a lifetime. We might have great intentions to print images from our digital cameras and mobile phones, but when we get back home other things crowd out life, and we forget.

It has also been suggested that a whole generation of history may be lost visually because photographs are not being printed these day. Whilst there are certainly many ways to save digital images, (the cloud, and social media for instance) having a physical copy gives you the choice of framing it, or making a gift of it to family and friends. Added to this, when you have a photograph taken onboard it is taken by a professional photographer with the equipment and resources to match. Very often the quality aboard can be compared with photographs taken in professional studios ashore.

Where Can I Get a Photograph Taken

Photography studios are set up around the ship for formal evenings, and there are often a few different photographers working with different backgrounds. Some of the backgrounds are very traditional, and others are designed for candid and informal shots. You can even go for the black and white sultry shots similar to what you might expect in a professional studio. The size of the cruise ship you are on, and the number of photographers onboard will determine the variety of backgrounds you can go for.

There are also plenty of other opportunities for photographs outside of formal events such as, when you embark or disembark on gangplanks and ports. When you go to onboard parties or special events, or even whilst you are walking around the ship.

Photo Gallery

Most cruise ships have a large gallery of photographs displayed on racks or in binders. As space is a premium many photographs may only be on display for a couple of days before being taken down to make way for others. Don't be too alarmed by this, as the photo department often have all of the images that have been taken throughout the cruise available for the duration of your time aboard. If you are on a particularly long cruise they may not be able to keep all images taken, but it is worth checking this with the photo department when you get aboard. Some of the newer ships have computers, which you can search through and request the image/images you want.

If you want some of your own images printing, most ships will accommodate you, and you can request an image to be printed from a few available sizes. Some cruise ships have machines you can insert a memory card into and select the sizes you would like. If this is not available often the photo team behind the counter will be able to accommodate your needs. You can also purchase cameras and other photography related ephemera at the gallery. Sometimes they have offers on cameras and albums, so don't always expect to pay a fortune.

Video

The sea shimmers an iridescent phthalo blue as light sparkles like faceted jewels off the rippling waves coming from the bow. You have seen places of sublime beauty, and cultures that stir up emotions that were once dormant. It has been a cruise of meditation, relaxation and a dream you simply must preserve. Then you get home and all is you see is shaky, hand held images of a bunch of passengers waving for 2 hours on the video you bought to preserve this memory.

I am not painting a good picture of cruise videos so far am I. However, I believe this perception of them is somewhat outdated – at least for quite a few companies anyway. This is because on most cruise ships these days, you have many people that have been trained professionally, or have come from a video background and know how to make a professional movie. I say movie, because that is what many cruise videos are like these days – purpose made to capture the cruise like a film or documentary. To do this, they have state of the art video cameras, editing suits, sound equipment, and a keen desire to show their worth.

Where Will the Video Be Shown?

Despite my edifying comments about the new breed of videographers aboard cruise ships, it should not be taken for granted that all cruise videos are good. Seeing what you are going to get before your purchase is essential if you don't want to be slitting your throat at the grotesque disturbing images of passengers waving and smiling. You can do this by turning your cabin television to a certain channel where you will be shown regular updates. (Ask at the photo/video department for what channel the video will be showing on, or just skip through the channels.)

How Will Your Video Come?

As technology changes the way you will receive the video will change over the forthcoming years. This means at the moment you may only get the choice of taking a DVD home from most ships. But going into the future you will be able to get a download, or you may be able to stream it to your computer.

Should You Buy the Video?

A well executed video can help remind you of your cruise like nothing else. This is especially the case if it has facts, information, and is similar to a documentary. Having said all that, I would be careful of sending even the most outstanding video as a gift to friends, it might not have the desired effect you were intending.

Tips

1. The photography shop can be good for buying discounted cameras.
2. Photo shoots can be a very busy time especially during formal evenings, and if you are wanting a few shots, or are after something a little different, it is worth having a talk with the photo manager to see what he/she can do. They may suggest another day, or organize a time when the venue will be quiet.
3. You will probably be asked to pose quite a lot for photos on the cruise, so expect to feel a little like you are being hunted by Paparazzi.
4. If you want to appear on the cruise video have a chat with the videographer, and they will make sure they film you and don't edit you out.
5. Special feature videos are often available on cruise ships, and they focus on a particular cruise itinerary. They are often cheaper if bought alongside the cruise video.
6. If you can't find your picture in the photo gallery, ask at the photo shop as they will generally know where to look because all photos as stored by date and event.

25

Onboard Activities

I must warn you that in the next 2 chapters I do run through a few lists now and again because it was the simplest way to identify activities aboard. When you see a list, rather than read through it, my suggestion would be to look at the ones that are pertinent to your needs – unless you are a list collector, then the next 2 chapters are perhaps the highlight of the book.

All ships offer different activities, so certainly don't expect everything I mention to be present on one particular ship. Cruise companies often provide activities based upon the age demographic they are trying to attract. Even in the same company you might see a large difference in activities aboard certain ships. Just because you have sailed on 'Robinson's Island', it doesn't mean you will have the same choice of activities on its sister ship, 'Robinson's Saver Island'. If shipboard activities are going to feature to some extent in your requirements, then it is important to look for a ship and company that will provide what you require.

Families & Children's Activities

There are ships that specifically cater for families and children, many even have particular areas devoted to children's entertainment. These areas are designated as safe zones, and have a dedicated staff and security to watch over the children. All crewmembers in these youth areas are immediately recognizable as they are often in bright, friendly looking clothes, and the security team look less intimidating than their counterparts who check your baggage and boarding card on entry to the ship. This facility leaves parents free to do something themselves, knowing that their children are safely occupied.

The activities for children are based upon age groups, and specific sections in the youth area are set up to accommodate each group. For the young children they have areas for reading, climbing, playing, sand pits and even places for them to sleep. For the older children the activities may include: mini-golf, table tennis, basketball, 3D movies, water slides, magic shows, sporting events, spa treatments, cooking lessons, water games, games consoles, writing classes, painting classes, and design classes to mention just a few. If you pick the right cruise for your family, the ship can provide so much entertainment children often don't want to leave the ship to explore destinations ashore.

Other Activities

Whilst resort style cruises seem to be geared towards families with children, this isn't necessarily their entire target market. Many adults choose the resort cruise because once they are aboard, the majority of activities are included in the price. It can be a veritable theme park on some ships because they offer things like zip lining, rock climbing, bowling, sword fencing, golf driving, surfing, ice skating and countless other activities. For something a little more relaxing they also offer a library, casinos, cigar smoking rooms, reading rooms, games room, meeting rooms, and a host of other rooms to relax in. In the evening you might fancy winding down by going to one of a number of shows, theatres, art auctions, shopping arcades, ice extravaganzas, or perhaps a disco.

Spa Cruise

Many of the new ships are actually designed in such a way to cater for the passenger who wants to have the spa as a focus of their cruise. Cabins can be rented that are linked to the spa and give private access to saunas, swimming pools, steam rooms, and a whole array of treatments. When you go on a cruise these days, you can quite literally return home feeling and looking very different. Judging by the Botox, teeth whitening, special colon irrigation, deep tissue massages, and the special dietary plans aboard, it appears you could be unrecognizable by the time you disembark.

One thing is for certain, this new energised, relaxed and physically different you, comes at a price. Whilst it might sound great splashing out on: acupuncture, body scrubs, facials, nail manicures, bikini wax's, thermal suit treatments, ice treatments, cosmetic surgery and an array of different massages whilst aboard, (these and more can be had aboard many cruise ships) it might not take long to undo all of your hard work (or should that be others hard work) when you get back at home. Those lines of worry, bags of tiredness or aches of stress will be hammering at your body remorselessly as you work to pay it all back.

Shopping

As with any truly rewarding vacation experience, a cruise will allow you plenty of opportunities to buy tat – sorry a slight slip there, I meant to say mementoes of your trip. These mementoes aren't just things like fridge magnets, new swimming costumes, clothes with the cruise logo on them, or a stick of rock (candy) - they can often be quite large purchases. For instance, you can buy a watch worth many thousands, a piece of glass worth a similar fortune, and a painting that is so expensive, the money could have been used as a down payment on a house.

Shops are often situated in a particular section of the ship that are sometimes called malls. In these malls you have jewellery shops, duty free shops, designer shops, gift shops and camera/photo shops. They even have a market aboard some cruise ships on certain days, and they sell off at discounted prices old stock from a previous cruise or cruises. This can be a good opportunity to grab a bargain, and depending on how long they have had the items, the saving can be substantial.

Many passengers use the the carrot of duty-free as an incentive to buy themselves something rather expensive. Be mindful that many countries have a limit to how much you can claim duty free when you are returning back to them. You may think you have saved a fortune, but when you declare it at customs on returning home, you may find you have to part an additional payment before you can take it into or out of a country. If the item you have bought is expensive, the duty you pay on it can be considerable.

Tips

1. Most shops aboard are generally closed whilst the ship is at port. This also applies to the casino, photo department and some other places aboard. The pools and activities centres are often open.
2. Markets onboard have special discounted prices as old stock from previous cruises is sold off.
3. Deals on spa treatments can be had if you go on a tour of their facilities when you first arrive aboard, and they will often hand you discount vouchers. You can also get cheaper deals when the ship is at port.
4. Youth areas are very different from cruise to cruise, and many cater for a variety of ages.
5. Security can be in place on some cruise ships to monitor children in certain sections of the ship. This can give parents the piece of mind to know their children will be safe whilst they enjoy another activity.
6. Don't expect that because you have sailed with a particular company before, you will be getting exactly the same in terms of facilities and activities on a different ship, because you generally won't. All ships have different activities aboard.
7. Special activities aboard such as zip lining, wave surfing and such like are becoming available with more cruise lines, but generally only on the very large ships.
8. Many cruise companies offer special access to spa facilities if you book certain cabins.

26

Add-ons & Specialist Cruises

The term add-ons, is something many of us are familiar with these days when it comes to mobile Apps, getting extra fries with a meal, and insurance policies. Cruise companies are no exception, and they too provide add-ons, but often they are just that little bit different.

You can get the add-on marriage, add-on renewal of your wedding vows, add-on honeymoon package, add-on meet a celebrity, and the add-on education lesson from some of the finest minds in the world. I don't think they have started add-on marriage counselling courses, add-on psychotherapist training, and add-on law degrees, although even these services may not be too far into the future.

To get many of these add-ons you can go on a traditional cruise, or if you want something just that little bit different, you can book specialist cruises.

Guest Speakers & Educational Cruises

Some guest speakers on cruise ships are well known celebrities who give talks highlighting their careers and lives. These are often free add-ons to your standard cruise, and are very well attended, so making sure you book early for these events as seating is often limited. Having said that, they will often repeat it over the course of a cruise, or you can watch the repeat on the ships TV throughout the cruise – but it isn't quite the same on the television is it?

On sea days you can often attend venues aboard to watch cooking displays, or listen to guest speakers that have risen to the top of their professions. These can include prominent politicians, producers, publishers, pilots, scientists, journalists, historians, actors, architects, astronauts, authors, explorers, directors, musicians, cooks, landscape designers and the list goes on. Some specialist cruises have tours that are led by these guest speakers.

Even if you don't book a specialist cruise, on almost all other cruise holidays there will be some aspect of education aboard such as: guest lectures, cooking classes, wine tasting lessons, cocktail mixing tutorials, dance classes, surfing lessons, rock climbing lessons, internet beginner/advanced classes, photography/video classes, web page design courses, writing courses, golf lessons, pottery classes, painting lessons, and even SCUBA (Self Contained Breathing Apparatus) diving courses. I personally attained all my qualifications for SCUBA diving on cruise ships.

You might be thinking that courses such as these will be making the cruise significantly more expensive, but actually many are free, and those you need to pay for can be a very cost effective way for passengers to learn something new. The SCUBA diving courses for instance are surprisingly inexpensive on some cruise ships, and can often be cheaper than their land based competitors. Obviously, you will need to factor into the price the cruise itself, but if you choose the right cruise it can work out cheaper than traveling to a country and then paying for a

SCUBA course.

Weddings/Renewing Vows

If you want that truly special occasion to be something different, and don't fancy getting married whilst falling from a plane, or having an Elvis impersonator preside over it, you might want to think of a having a cruise wedding. As well as having an idyllic location and honeymoon included, you may also have a captain to preside over the ceremony.

Getting married or renewing your vows can be surprisingly inexpensive for couples on a cheap budget, although it may reduce the number of family and friends that can come – which could be a positive or a negative, depending on your relationship with them.

Specialist Cruises

When we think of cruising, many of us immediately are reminded of large ocean going ships that accommodate thousands of passengers. Even the opening forward to this book focuses on the transatlantic cruising of the 19th and early part of the 20th century on the large ocean going ships. However, other cruises were taking place at the same time in places such as Egypt, along the Nile.

As you can imagine, those early forays in to cruising have been expanded, and you can take river cruises in many places around the world. This leisurely, and more intimate way to experience a place, and culture, is becoming ever more popular. These cruises have a more intimate feel about them, and the décor onboard can enhance the mood and feel of the cruise. You can even have murder mystery cruises, where everyone aboard is involved.

There are also specialist cruises for those that have and interest in archaeology, architecture, and history. Cruises that explore the polar regions, or very remote areas. These ships are generally purpose built for the extreme conditions, and scientists will be available onboard to give lectures, and answer any questions you may have. Some very large cruise ships have sails that are put up when the ship is out at sea. They give the feeling of being on a large sailing ship, only there is no need to sleep in a hammock, or climb up and down rigging.

If you feel you can get enough people together, you can even book a whole cruise ship for your party, and make the cruise as bespoke as you like. Lesbian, Gay, Bisexual, Transgender, Queer, Intersexual, Asexual, Pansexual, Kinks + (LGBTQIAPK+) being examples of a groups I have seen do this.

What I am essentially saying is, work out what you are after from a cruise, and book one accordingly. The chances are, you will find one to suit your needs, and if you can't, then perhaps you could organise your own. With a trend for people to experience lasting memories, instead of owning excessive amount of trappings – golden memories instead of gold, that sort of thing; cruise companies are becoming ever more diverse in what they offer.

So, if you are after an add-on with a difference, or

even a different type of cruise, there are many things you could consider when it comes to cruising. By looking for interesting add-ons, you might actually add-on to your knowledge, and expertise, or even add-on an experience that stays with you a lifetime, which is certainly something you could tick off your bucket list.

Tips

1. Specialised cruises that offer educational talks are often no more expensive than a standard cruise.
2. Specialist talks by well known people are often free to access, but room constraints may dictate how many can attend.
3. Specialist cruises often focus on one area and explore it in detail. For instance, it could be a cruise exploring the Hebridean islands, fjords in Norway or the Antarctic.
4. Having a renewal of vows ceremony is quite popular on cruise ships these days, and is generally very inexpensive.
5. If you are visiting lots of ports, the educational activities may be less, but most evenings you will find some available.
6. Taking a SCUBA diving course whilst aboard can be a great way to make your cruise that little bit different. It can be very cost effective, and might even be cheaper than flying to another country to do it.
7. Weddings are very common on cruise ships and can be quite inexpensive. Obviously, it might be more of an intimate affair with fewer people, but that might fit in with your desires a little more. Added to this, cruise companies also offer excellent photography and video packages aboard.

27

Safety

Modern cruising is extremely safe, and satellite mapping systems can plot weather patterns as they appear on the oceans, which means cruise ships can steer themselves out of dangerous weather conditions. Added to this, modern cruise ships have design features, such as bulkheads and watertight doors, which stop a breach in a hull from sinking the ship. If a fire were to break out in the engine room it would be sealed off, and carbon dioxide would be pumped into the space to suffocate the flames. Added to this, safety drills are a constant factor onboard in one form or another for crewmembers. Personally, I would say it has never been a safer time in history to take a cruise.

Despite the excellent safety record of cruise ships they can still get into trouble on occasions, and being prepared is always paramount. Because of this, passengers are expected to understand what to do in an emergency. In this chapter I am going to look at safety, its impact upon the passenger, and at some of the safety equipment you will find aboard. My hope is that you will never need to use these in the event of an emergency, but if you do, at least you will have more of an idea what is available to you, having read this chapter.

Muster Station

Muster stations are areas of the ship that are easily

accessible for all, and relatively close to the waterline (on deck 7 for instance). They are usually in large spaces where people can congregate together such as, restaurants, casino's, and theatres.

For emergencies and drills, you need to make sure you go to the correct muster station as a passenger. There are often several muster stations on a large cruise ship, and each are generally identified by a letter in the alphabet. Identifying what muster station you need to go to is very easy because it is often printed on your cabin card, life jacket, on a sticker on your cabin wall. If you are unsure of where your personal muster station is, you can also ask a member of the crew, and they will be able to tell from your cabin number. This is because your muster station is generally positioned below your cabin, and if you take an imaginary knife and slice down vertically through the ship from your cabin, whichever large area it cuts through on a lower deck is generally where it will be positioned – although not always.

Muster Drill

It is part of maritime law for all passengers to attend the main muster drill, which is usually before the ship sails. You will hear an announcement made over the sound system aboard asking you to make your way to your muster station. You may or may not be required to go back to your cabin to pick up life jackets, but you will be made aware of this in an announcement.

The objective of a muster drill is to make all passengers aware of where they need to be, what they need to take with them, and what they need to do in the event of an emergency aboard. The actual drill is not generally a long protracted affair, and often lasts less than half an hour. In the announcement the captain or a member of the bridge will highlight where to find emergency equipment, and what to do in the event of an emergency aboard. They will also ask you to bring warm clothes, a life jacket and your family (if you have one) with you to the designated station in a real emergency.

Lifejackets

You will find lifejackets in your cabin, and these are generally under your bed, or above the wardrobe. They are often huge orange blocks of Styrofoam and looking at them may have you concluding that they have all the style of a shipping container, and in essence are like wearing one. It seems strange to me that a ship full of technological advancements would still be using these cumbersome objects if we find ourselves in the ocean thousands of miles away from civilisation, but then they do have a whistle and a light I suppose.

If you do have to take a life jacket to the drill don't wear it until you are asked to do so because passengers have been known to have horrific accidents when wearing them. Make sure you pick up any trailing straps as the are incredibly easy to trip on, especially going up and down stairs.

Other Safety Equipment

You perhaps may never have the opportunity to experience much of the other safety equipment on a cruise ship, and hopefully not for the purpose it was intended. The Life Raft for instance is one such item you may only actually see stored in a large fiberglass cylinder on the decks. Lifeboats on the other hand are items of safety that you will not only see, but quite possibly have the opportunity to experience. This is because if you are on a ship that can not moor up against the shore, they will often use lifeboats to transport you and other passengers including crew ashore. Lifeboats are numerous on a modern cruise ship, and you can rest assured the capacity of all lifeboats and life rafts on the ship is far more than the number of passengers the ship holds. Any images you have in your mind of waving goodbye to your nearest and dearest because of room restrictions on them, is out of the question.

Many lifeboats can carry over 350 people, so imagine how ill everyone will be as it pitches and tosses in the large waves. That is why you will not be given food or drink for a substantial period of time in the lifeboat. If you are expecting gammon slices to be carved up, and endless bottles of cola to be handed out to everyone, think again. You will simply be given a seasickness pill and a small amount of water whilst aboard – unless your time on a lifeboat stretches into days I suppose, but this is very unlikely given the technology these days.

Oh, I almost forgot to say; there sometimes aren't any

toilets on a lifeboat either, which means that you will have to eject waste over the side – now that would be a cruise to write home about.

Tips

1. Life jackets are often kept under a bed or on top of a wardrobe. If there aren't enough to cover every occupant inside your cabin, contact the pursers' desk to send some more for you. There should also be lifejackets that will fit your children.
2. Bringing warm clothes with you in your luggage is important because it gets cold even in warm climates, and sitting on a lifeboat in thin garments would not be comfortable.
3. Despite the likelihood of an incident requiring safety equipment being very remote on a cruise, make sure you attend the drill, even if you have been to them before. This is because every ship is slightly different, and safety equipment is stowed in different places.
4. Listening at the muster drill is important, but don't expect to remember everything that is said.
5. Never put life jackets on whilst walking to a drill because if you fall wearing a life jacket, it can be more damaging to you than not wearing one.
6. Cold-shock is what you get when you jump into cold water from a warm environment. It can often kill people in a few minutes as the body can't adjust to the cold temperature quickly. Wearing a warm jumper will help to lessen that reaction to some extent, which could be enough to save your life in an emergency.

28

Time

You are probably thinking why are we discussing time because the point of going away on vacation is so that I can forget time schedules and relax. Unfortunately, when you take a cruise, you can't just forget about time altogether because it essentially dictates your whole cruise. In actuality you have taken a vacation to be in an environment where your time will be dictated by time obsessed timekeepers – especially if the ship is crossing time zones.

Whilst aspects of this chapter may be a little tongue in cheek at times, I can quite honestly say, this is one of the most important chapters in this guidebook. This is because it might actually prevent you from missing the ship, which would prove to be catastrophic, both in financial terms, and in stress levels. I have missed the ship on one occasion, but thankfully I managed to get aboard a pilot boat, which took me to the ship before it left the area for 2 weeks. If this hadn't happened I would have had to catch flight to meet up with the ship, or stay in a hotel until it returned.

Having the Right Time

On a cruise, you need to know the time you are supposed to be present for dinner, what times you can book tours, what time your tour will be leaving, what time you need to be back to the ship, what time formal time starts, what time shows start, what time the shops open and close, what time to expect your steward in the morning, what time the medical centre opens, what time the ship is using – ship time or shore time, and what time I will stop reeling off this endless list of times.

Whilst you perhaps appreciate it is important to have the right time on you at all times on a cruise, there can be a problem when it comes to certain cruises. On some cruises, you might think that you have the right time on you, but in actuality you are working from the wrong time. How could this happen? It often happens because of things called time zones (time zones are imaginary lines drawn around the earth splitting time into 24 parts, and start at Greenwich England). Some ships change their time onboard to accommodate the change of time as they sail over time zones, whilst other ships have a set time they work off throughout the cruise, meaning the ships time will always be constant. (This time is usually taken from the initial port the ship has sailed from.) Either way, this can cause problems for passengers on a cruise, as each has its positives and negatives, depending upon on whether you are on the ship or ashore.

Ship Time & Shore Time

Some cruise ships don't want the passengers to be concerned that the ship is moving over time zones, and because of this, they use the time from the original port the ship sailed from. This means that everything on that cruise revolves around a set standard time – and this includes everything ashore, such as tours. As you can imagine, having one set time works very well onboard because both passengers and crew don't have to constantly change their watch or timepiece whenever they cross over a time zone. But it can make it difficult when passengers and crew go ashore. This is because when you go ashore the time you have been using aboard will be different to the country you are in, which can get a little confusing at times – let me explain.

If your watch stops or loses time whilst you are ashore, you have nothing to compare it with, as all other times will be different to what you are using. Theoretically, unless you know the time difference from ship time to the local port time, you could be in trouble. Whilst this might sound like a simple thing to work out, passengers and crew sometimes don't know what the difference is between ship time and shore time, and end up missing the ship. Most of the problems seem to occur when passengers and crew are working off a watch that is losing time and because they have nothing to compare it to ashore, they don't realise the watch is losing time. When they arrive back at the port they are confronted with seeing a cruise ship on the horizon steaming away to another port. I have seen both passengers and crew miss the ship on many occasions because of not having the accurate time on them.

If the ship does the opposite and keeps to local time (the time of the port the ship is stopping at) for both ship time and shore time, then other complications arise. This is because if the ship is regularly sailing over time zones, failure to adjust your timepiece daily could mean you disembark the ship working off the wrong time, which could ultimately mean missing the ship. On some cruises you can go over so many time zones you can become quite confused as to what time it should be.

But I can hear you saying, 'at least you can always check what the correct time is when you are ashore.' But unfortunately most people don't realise they need to check the time of each port and many find themselves working off the previous day's time on their watch, oblivious it is an hour or two different from the actual time. Once again it can lead to missing the ship.

Combination Time

To try and combat this and make things 'easier' for all aboard, some cruise ships have tried using a combination of the both, by having ship time for all activities aboard, and shore time for everything that is done ashore. Rather than make things easier, it can confuse everyone completely, because it is throwing too many variables into the metaphorical pot. With this system no one quite knows what time is supposed to be used for what, when a specific time is supposed to change, which one of the two times is being used for departure, or if they can remember which watch was actually being used for what time. Heaven help you if you don't carry a bag full of timepieces, or take a degree in cartography to work out longitude and latitude differences.

Mobile Phones & Time

Many of the problems I have highlighted thus far can

be addressed by taking a mobile phone with you ashore. This is because mobile phones will often pick up the local time where you are positioned on the planet. You should be able to arrive at a country and check the exact time wherever you are, and even check the time of the original port you departed from. That is why whenever I go ashore, I always carry a mobile phone with me as a secondary source of time.

Make sure your mobile phone is charged prior to leaving the ship. Using satnav facilities can eat up battery life on mobile phones, and you need to make sure you have enough power should you need to call the ship (always take the ships phone number with you when ashore).

When ashore it is always a good idea to be aware of time, even if you are not going through time zones. Missing the ship is something that can be expensive, is very disruptive and is easily done.

Remember – the captain will not generally wait for a passenger that is running late unless you are on a cruise organised tour.

Tips

1. Carrying 2 timepieces with you will always mean you will be able to corroborate the time, (watch and Mobile for instance) if you are traveling on your own.
2. Don't trust city or town clocks because clocks in cities are often wrong, and passengers have been caught out using local clocks to adjust their own timepiece.
3. Check your timepiece before leaving the ship.
4. Charge up your mobile phone before leaving the ship, especially if you are using it as a timepiece.
5. Don't always trust other people when it comes to getting the right time. I nearly missed the ship on 2 occasions because inaccurate times given to me by others.
6. Buying an expensive timepiece in some countries can be a problem unless you buy it from a recommended and reputable company. Some shops have been known to show you a quality watch, and when they pack it away they replace it for something of a similar weight but far less value, like a brick.
7. Take the ship contact number with you when you go ashore. It doesn't necessarily mean if you are running late they will wait for you, but at least you and the captain will be on the same page.

29

Where to Go

Perhaps the most common question I am asked a is, 'what is your favourite place out of all the ones you have visited?' As this book isn't to talk about me, however much I would like that opportunity, I need to reference this question to assist in helping you with your cruising experiences. So here is a thinly veiled attempt to alert you to some cruises I have been on that might interest you.

The World Cruise

If you have the time and resources, I would highly recommend a world cruise because you will almost certainly have an opportunity to experience aspects of the world like few other forms of travel. I have flown to Australia many times, but when I visited it on a world cruise it felt completely different in every respect. I felt like I was connecting to the country in a similar way to those early explorers like Captain Cook, despite the opulent nature of a cruise ship. This is because you get a certain back to basics feel as you connect to each country trough the gradual introduction of wildlife on the oceans, from Albatross as they follow the ship, to whales, dolphins and eventually seals the nearer to land you get. It also helped me to reference one country to another, and see how they were tied through trade, culture, language and ultimately the oceans.

In my opinion it is important to go on a slightly smaller cruise ship, (24,000 to 50,000 Gross Tonnage GT) because there are many more possibilities for it to stop at small ports. Obviously the amount of time you spend in each place is very short, but it can provide a perfect opportunity for you to see if you would like to explore that country in more depth on a future occasion. Having said that, some cruise ships have specialised tours that leave the ship for a few days and explore inland areas such as, the Andes Mountain Range and Machu Picchu, the Great Wall of China, Uluru (Airs Rock), the Galapagos Islands, Angkor Watt and many others. This makes it a surprisingly effective way to see a large section of the world that can sometimes be expensive to visit if done individually.

If you are thinking that a world cruise is a little out of your budget even if you take a small cabin, don't lose heart. I have seen some very cheap deals for world cruises crop up now and again – although they might have required the occasional ships furnace to be stocked with coal, come to think of it.

Amazon

Large ships (not the super sized cruise ships) can sail the Amazon River to Manaus the capital city of the Amazonas. This is perhaps one of the most fascinating cruises you will ever have an opportunity to experience. Depending on where the cruise departs, will determine the length of an Amazon cruise, however, expect it to take about 2-weeks.

The cruise usually stops at different villages along the

Amazon River for passengers to get a feel of the native culture. Despite having the occasional cruise ship visiting them, the local villages are not tourist traps by any means, and many have an authenticity about them. Sailing for days down this vast expanse of water and absorbing its smells, experiencing its wildlife, and engaging with the wilderness, is something you will never forget.

The Black Sea/Baltic

The cruises around the Baltic, Black Sea, or Eastern Europe are in my mind a little out of the ordinary. Unfortunately, because of situations in the world, some of the very popular destinations are no longer frequented by cruise ships. This is a real shame as the cultures are so diverse and full of splendour like few others. However, when one destination is removed the cruise companies often to replace it with something of equal interest. Places like Bulgaria, Romania, Estonia and Croatia have a wealth of history, and the cities and towns are like few others I have ever seen for architecture.

Cruise ships travel between April and September in this area, although there are exceptions. The temperatures between July and August are the warmest, but they are also the busiest times of year for cruise ships. Despite this, even in these periods you will not find many of the towns and cities anywhere near as congested as some other cruise destinations.

Alaska

Alaska is one of those places that lends itself well to a cruise. This is because you can explore the fjords and experience ice calfing (or calving) from huge glaciers. You can also go on tours to see the extensive wildlife it is so renowned for, such as whales, orcas, seals, bears, eagles, otters, and the list goes on. You can have some truly close encounters with Alaskan wildlife like nowhere else I have experienced in the world. You can also go on some wonderful exploration tours with husky sledge rides, or fly over glaciers in planes and helicopters, and experience the majesty of it all.

Picking what months you should visit Alaska by cruise ship can be a little tricky though. This is because there is more wildlife later in the year between July and October, (as animals feed on the vast shoals of salmon that are running up rivers) but the weather is a little more unpredictable at this time of year with lots of rain. Despite this, I would suggest any time of year is better than not seeing it at all, and if you can't get the dates you want, you will still find it to be a fascinating experience.

Caribbean

The Caribbean is a very diverse area and has some of the most outstanding beaches you can imagine. The fact that it is spread over 7000 islands with 13 sovereign island nations, and something in the region of 12 independent territories, means each island offers something that little bit different. The food on the Caribbean has influences from around the world, and many islands have their own take on local dishes. Much of the Caribbean is also geared towards large cruise ships, and beautiful beaches are only a short walk from the main ports.

I have visited much of the Caribbean over the years and it never loses its charm and charisma. Despite it being a holiday mecca for cruise ships, for some reason it doesn't seem crowded - for the most part anyway. Added to this, the weather is generally fantastic, unless you are unfortunate enough to catch a hurricane that is.

There are of course many other cruises you can go on such as: Eastern and Western Mediterranean cruises, Norwegian Fjord cruises, European river cruises, Nile cruises, Transatlantic cruises, Atlantic Island cruises, and Canada New England cruises, to name but a few. If nothing else, the ones I have briefly highlighted might get your mouth watering with anticipation when deciding where to go on a cruise.

Tips

1. Recommendations are certainly worth getting from friends and family. Also there are many sites on the internet that will go through point by point what to expect on a particular cruise.
2. Take opportunities when you can to see a place, because you never know what the future holds for certain counties.
3. Autumn cruises are simply magnificent in some parts of the world, and foliage on trees can be exquisite like in Canada and New England. There is also an increased migration of animals this time of year, making your chances of encountering wildlife that much more probable.
4. High season may be the only time available for you to take a cruise due to work, and family commitments, but being a little more flexible in where you go can help to keep costs down.
5. Learn a few words of the local language before you disembark in countries, because it is amazing how much of a difference it makes to your experience.
6. Cruising can introduce you to islands, which you might not have a chance to see any other way. I have seen Easter Island, Tahiti, the Cook Islands, Papua New Guinea and so much more because of cruising. You can obviously get to these places by plane, but seeing them by ship can be special, and sometimes it can be cheaper.

30

Secrets About Crew Life

Explaining aspects of crew life in one small chapter is perhaps too much of an ask, and I suspect a whole book should be devoted to this subject. In the few brief pages that will follow, I will try to touch on a few significant aspects of the crewmembers' life, work, accommodation, and relationships. The subjects I discuss are based upon some of the most popular questions I have been asked over the years. If you are after a no holes bared look at what life is like for crewmembers aboard cruise ships, I would suggest you read my memoir entitled, Robinson Cruising – an unashamed plug there!

Contract/Career

The cruise ship contract for many crewmembers varies depending upon their position aboard. For instance, captains and some officers work 4-month contracts, and have 1 or 2 months leave in-between ships. Shop workers, photo/video, casino, spa etc. generally work between 6 and 8 month contracts. The other employees onboard, such as stewards, cleaners, restaurant department, laundry, and deck hands, generally have 8 month contracts, with 2 months off.

Many crewmembers do not get paid when on leave from the ship, but many don't generally need to pay taxes on their wages if they are away from your country for a significant percentage of the year either, which balances things out somewhat. (What taxes you pay if any are determined by the laws of the country the crewmember is based in.)

Cabins

The type of cabin a crewmember is assigned to is very much dependent upon his/her position aboard the ship. The captain and officers have different degrees of quality cabins dependent upon the stripes on their shoulders, however, most officers have their own personal cabin. The rest of the crew generally live lower down on the ship, and share cabins with other crewmembers. Generally speaking, crew who work for the same department share cabins together.

Most crew cabins are small, have no windows, are beneath the waterline, and can accommodate more than one person. On some cruise ships, crew cabins could be 170sq ft/16sq ft and occupy 4 people, whilst sharing the ablutions room with an adjoining cabin. This means upwards of 8 people could be using 1 washroom. (This is becoming less common on the modern cruise lines.) Lack of space often restricts too many items being placed in the rooms apart from beds and wardrobes, but often a small desk and chair is present in the corner of a cabin. To give each crewmember some privacy in their bunk, curtains are also provided to run alongside their beds.

Officers have a steward that is paid by the company to make sure their cabin is clean and tidy, and clothes are washed. Nearly all other crewmembers clean their own cabins, and just to make sure they are cleaning them to a certain standard, weekly inspections are held by officers. If it is found a cabin does not pass inspection, the crewmember can be disciplined. This discipline may include, reduced time for shore leave, or in extreme cases, being discharged from service on that ship.

Relationships

Sexual relationships between crew and passengers is not permitted on most cruise ships as far as I am aware. If a crewmember is found in a passenger's cabin and it has not been authorised, the crewmember can be dismissed off the ship. This might sound a little harsh, but it is to safeguard passengers and crew in case allegations are made about sexual misconduct.

Relationships between crewmembers is permitted and you will find many crewmembers are either in a relationship, or are keen on finding one. Unfortunately, because of time spent away from home and the lifestyle onboard, many crewmembers have failed marriages. Even if crewmembers don't have extramarital relationships aboard, their partners back home may leave them for someone else because of the lack of time spent with each other.

Most relationships that start on cruise ships fail to last a couple of contracts because it is sometimes not possible for couples to get on the same ship together. It also doesn't follow that they will get a cabin together, which makes it difficult to have a relationship. In these instances, many couples have to organise with colleagues to vacate rooms if they want time alone.

Facilities/Entertainment

On many cruise lines, those working as officers, in the entertainment department, shops, spa and photography departments can use passenger facilities to some degree, but this is very much dependent upon the cruise line and their policies. On the larger ships, crew have access to their own swimming pool, gyms and socialising areas. They also have a crew bar, where regular events and parties take place, such as Karaoke, discos, band nights, gaming evenings and such like. Keeping crewmembers entertained in one form or another is deemed very important by most cruise companies, because they realise it keeps up moral in what are often intense working environments.

Eating Mess

There are often at least 2 designated eating areas for crewmembers on a ship; the Officers Mess (Ward Room) and the general Crew Mess Deck. Food in the Officers Mess is very similar to what passengers eat, and they have a steward waiting on tables. In the Crew Mess Deck, food is generally buffet style, and it caters in choice for the many different cultures that are working aboard. Unlike the Officers Mess, no dress code is required for the Crew Mess.

This is the briefest of brief insights into crew life. If you should find yourself wanting to know more ask a crewmember when you get aboard or you could just read my book Robinson Cruising – 2 unashamed plugs in one chapter, its unforgivable.

Tips

1. Crew and passenger fraternisation is frowned upon these days because it is not considered professional conduct to do so. It can also have some far more serious consequences if a crewmember is accused of abusing a passenger, or vice versa.
2. It can be a dismissing offence if a crewmember is found in a passenger cabin without the consent of the ships captain or pursers' department.
3. Passenger organised tours take crewmembers to help assist the guide.
4. If a crewmember is late for the ship, unless he/she is the Doctor, the Chief Engineer or the Captain, the ship may leave without them.
5. Crew messes (eating areas) occupy different parts of the ship, and they are usually lower down or below the waterline.
6. Selected crew can eat in some passenger areas, but this is entirely dependent upon what protocols are in place for a certain cruise line.
7. Crew cabins are generally below the water line, and are often occupied by more than one person.
8. Officer cabins have a steward and one occupant, unless they have a partner aboard.
9. Couples that are working on the same ship may not be able to get a cabin together.

31

Small Island

People often liken cruise ships to cities because of their size and the number of facilities aboard, but from an early age I always though of them as floating islands. This is in part because I remember thinking a cruise ship was an island when I first saw one out on the ocean as a child. It is also to do with the fact that they seem to embody more physical aspects of an island than most cities. They are similar sizes to some islands, are surrounded by water, have small watercraft on their peripheries, and are governed by nature, and the environment to a large extent. This view was cemented some years later when I started working on cruise ships. I soon realised that it wasn't necessarily only the physical nature of them that was reminiscent of an island, but the culture and language that was evident aboard.

For instance, they have laws, which has evolved from their isolation from the mainland over many hundreds of years. They also have a language, (an example of this is in chapter 34) which has evolved over thousands of years. They have one leader whose word is law, and failure to comply with the 'chief' will have you feeling the consequences immediately. When the captain makes his/her decision there is no questioning, negotiating because their word is law and that is the end of the matter. (Although that aspect of them is perhaps more akin to ancient islands that had chiefs.)

Statistics

It can certainly be said that the modern cruise liner is becoming ever larger, and in that respect they are physically starting to resemble islands more than ever before. With this in mind I thought I would run through a few statistics on some of the very latest and largest cruise ships in the world (without naming any of these ships because it is not relevant to this exercise). At this point I could easily give you their average height, weight, passenger numbers, cabin numbers, food intake, and any other statistic that are so readily available on cruise ships these days, but what would be the fun in that? As I love comparisons, I thought I would throw in a few at this point so you can get a feel for certain aspects of the modern cruise ship.

If you are a mathematician or an expert in working out statistics and see any variance in what I have worked out, please don't contact me because I don't give a pink feathered, blue tailed fig. Whilst I have done my best to be accurate, I may be out ever so slightly, especially in mouse numbers. Whilst accuracy is important in aspects of this book, this is not one of them – it is just for a bit of fun.

Height

It might surprise you to know that the height of some of the largest cruise ships from keel to funnel would be like standing on the head of the Statue of Liberty, in the clock at Big Ben, in the Whispering Dome of St Paul's Cathedral, or if you went to Venice, you would be towering above the whole city.

Length

The very large cruise ships are nearly one and a half times the length of the Titanic, 3 Giant Redwoods laid end to end, 21 Viking Long Boats, 36 Giant Anacondas, and the Eifel Tower would fit length ways inside one (it would probably have to be squashed at the bottom though). I am not sure how the French would feel about that?

Weight

The weight of a cruise ship is that of 1,240 Blue Whales, 1,500 average houses, 45,000 Elephants, 112,500 average cars, 2,045,454 people and 10,714,285,714 mice, although I might be out by 1 or 2 on that calculation.

Features

They have enough electric cable to wrap around Britain length ways from Scotland to the south coast of England 5 times, or around New York 70,000 times, or the same cable would take you half way to the moon. It would take 10 days to use up an Olympic sized swimming pool full of diesel if motoring full steam. The average meat eating person would have to live for 200 years to consume the same amount of meat that is eaten on a cruise in a single week. It would require 21 standard baths to hold the wine that is consumed in a week, and there are enough pizzas being consumed in one week that if stood end to end they would reach the height of the empire state building and nearly return half way back down (and that is only what is eaten by the crew).

There are other facts that I could have extrapolated, but I think you get the picture. Cruise ships are not only large and heavy; they have lots of everything aboard. Whether this is something that fills you in awe of what can be done by humankind, or it irritates you because so much of our finite resources are being used just to take us on vacation, is another question. It is perhaps one that is better left to a discussion over a nice drink, although perhaps not 21 baths of it.

Sufficient to say, cruise ships are certainly large enough to be classed as islands and who knows, they may even take on island status one day as they become completely independent from other cultures and countries. When this happens they may even have their own education facilities, and offer university degrees and such like.

I suppose the only question that needs to be asked is; what would they call these new supersized cruise ships? My suggestion would be 'Robinson's Island', although I would wouldn't I.

32

Top Tips for First Time Cruisers

I hope these final tips help you a little, and if there is something you need further clarification on, you can refer back to that particular section and read it again.

Things to Consider Before Your Cruise

1. For your first cruise, think about using a travel agent because it takes much of the stress out of organising a cruise. You will probably feel more confident after your first cruise to to do more of your own research, and you may be inclined to design your cruise around your specific needs and requirements.
2. Think about choosing a short cruise if you have not cruised before because you might not like it.
3. Certain travel agents provide bespoke cruises that can also include social activities. This can be a good option if you are traveling alone, or if you would like to make new friends.
4. Think of your requirements, and choose a cruise that suits you, don't just go for the deal.
5. An all inclusive deal has different meanings, and it is important to check exactly what you get for what you are paying. It may be that only certain beverages are included, or perhaps none at all. It could also mean that you may have to pay an

additional 15% (or more) gratuity per day for any services you receive.

6. None mainstream passengers may have a supplement to pay for a double or a twin, but more cruise ships are being built that have single cabins, and ones designed for people with disabilities. You may have to book early it get what you require though.
7. Decide whether you want a resort cruise where activities aboard take centre stage, or a port focused cruise where visiting destinations is the focus. Some cruise companies try to compromise between the two, which can work very well.
8. If you go on a resort cruise, many of the activities aboard will be factored in to the price of the cruise, and your outlay can be considerably less.
9. None resort cruise ships may still have lots of activities onboard, but you may not have the time to fully utilise them.
10. Take cash to pay for taxis, car parks, and such like. Factor in small denominations for tips in a currency that is accepted.
11. Exchanging a small amount of currency before you leave home can be helpful to pay for things when you first arrive, but weigh up how much cash you actually want to carry with you.
12. Take a carry on bag for all items you will require when you don't have your cases. You will not have access to your cases when you embark and the last evening before disembarking. If you are using your carry on bag for hand luggage on a plane, you will

need to know what liquids you can carry inside.

13. Book well in advance if there is a particular cruise you want to take as last minute deals might not include them. Cruise companies often advertise 12/18 months in advance of the cruise, and you can save substantial sums by booking early.
14. Use the ships plan for choosing a cabin, and remember noise, light, fresh air, and position, are key factors to keep in mind.
15. If you are flying to a cruise think about going a day early, and book a hotel near to the port. Flights can be delayed, and you may miss the ship or have a stressful time trying to catch it.
16. Read all the information provided by the cruise company/agent, and especially the cruise contract as it will identify exactly what you get.
17. Make sure all family members have passports with at least 6 months on them before taking a cruise.
18. Leave the ships details with family and friends so they can contact you in an emergency. Don't rely upon them being able to contact your mobile phone.
19. Make sure you have all the official and relevant paperwork for any children you may be taking.
20. Print a hard copy of all the paperwork to take with you, and make photocopies of any passports and other relevant documents. This is particularly advantageous if you are going to hire transport ashore.
21. Attach quality luggage tags to your cases, so the crew know who the case belongs to.

22. If you are organising your own transport to the cruise, book shuttles and taxis in advance. If you are driving to the ship, make sure you have somewhere to park, and be aware it can be quite expensive.
23. Pack adapters and multiple sockets so you can use your electrical items aboard.
24. Make sure your insurance covers you properly – remembering to include specific add-ons you might want for things such as, jet skiing, riding a scooter/motorbike, and extreme sports etc.

Arriving Onboard

25. Remember that most cruise ships are huge. Look at the plans of the ship on the companies' website or in their brochures, and get a rough idea of where everything is. Even when you get aboard you will still feel overawed a little, but don't worry about this, you can always ask others, and in a surprisingly short period of time you will know the ship very well.
26. You will probably be very tired after all the traveling, so take some time to rest before drills are called. If you go onto the top deck you can eat something small, and get a feel for what the cruise is going to be like.
27. Try to make it to the Sailaway party after drills, (it is usually in the top deck) as you will see the ship depart, and there may be free alcohol to celebrate.

Tours

28. Tours can be booked on the ship, but do this early on in the cruise, as some fill very quickly. You can also organise tours from some ships TV's, or with apps provided by the company.
29. If you organise your own excursions, the ship may not wait if you are late. Going with a cruise organised tour means the ship will wait for it to return.
30. You can often cancel a tour 24 to 48 hours before it departs, but find out first.
31. Know what time all aboard is, and make sure you have the right time.
32. You can make use of the ships facilities, such as the eateries, swimming pools, libraries, youth areas, and spa for instance, when the ship is at a port. To attract business on these days, you may even find the spa has special deals. There are also fewer people aboard using these facilities. But many places are also closed, or at least some aspect of them, such as casinos, bars, shops.
33. Lectures explaining ports and what to expect ashore are often given in the evenings. These lectures will explain places of interest, where banks and shops are situated, and you can ask questions throughout. This lecture can also be watched on your cabin TV on most cruise ships.
34. Booking a cruise tour with meals included can be expensive, but you may find a similar tour without food included at a much cheaper price.

Formal Evenings

35. Not all cruise ships have formal evenings, but for the ones that do, 6 o'clock is generally when formal time starts.
36. Every cruise company has different rules on what they expect in regards to the formal attire. You may be able to rent formal clothes aboard, which will reduce what you need to carry in your luggage.

Food

37. Inclusive restaurants are generally 1st and 2nd sitting, and you will need to choose which one you want to go to at the beginning of a cruise. Flexi dining/open seating means you can sit anywhere, and with whom you like; this option is becoming more common these days.
38. Food is generally included in the price of the cruise, but not speciality restaurants and some other treats.
39. Check what drinks are included in your deal, because it may only be tap water.
40. Tap water is generally good quality on cruise ships, and you can add lemon, or lime to it, to improve the taste. Always check that tap water is suitable to drink before consuming any.

Tipping/Gratuity

41. Gratuity is charged by most cruise companies and can sometimes be paid before joining a cruise.
42. Don't feel obliged to double tip, but if you want to specifically reward a crewmember for exceptional service, whatever you give them is acceptable.
43. Anywhere between 10 – 20% is standard for most gratuity and tip deductions.
44. Take small amounts of cash for tips. This is especially important when you go ashore.

Cabins

45. What cabin you get can often determine how much gratuity you pay. (Larger cabin = greater gratuity payment or tips.)
46. Many cabins are very small, and having lots of cases can reduce the space considerably. Cases that fit inside each other, or have soft sides are very good because they can fit underneath beds or in cupboards easier.
47. Keep all valuables in your safe including passports, remembering to take them with you ashore, and most importantly empty the safe before you leave.
48. If you have a noisy neighbour, speak to the Pursers desk rather than getting into a possible fracas with another passenger.

Safety

49. Drills will take place before your first departure, and you may or may not need to take a life jacket with you (some cruise lines don't require passengers to try on life jackets during the drill). Don't wear your life jacket until requested, as it can be dangerous walking and climbing stairs with them on.
50. Make sure there is a life jacket in your cabin for all the family.
51. Know your muster station position, and attend the drill at the beginning of the cruise.

Sickness

52. Seasickness is not very common on cruise ships, but taking medication with you aboard is advisable unless you know you will be OK. You can also get medication aboard, and it can be free.
53. Any visit to the medical centre can be expensive, and if you require medication take ample supplies.
54. Make sure your insurance covers you for every eventuality on a cruise. You may have to pay for treatments aboard, but you should be able to claim any medical costs incurred aboard from your insurance provider.
55. The medical centre is available 24/7 but it is generally only occupied at certain times of the day. These time are generally displayed on the main medical centre door.

Money

56. Keep an eye on how much you are spending throughout the cruise. This can be done either through your cabin TV, (logging into the appropriate channel) or by contacting the Pursers desk.
57. There are ATM machines aboard, but it can be expensive to use them.
58. The last evening of the cruise is usually a frantic rush of people paying their cruise bills. You can organise your final bill prior to that time to avoid standing in queues. Keeping an eye on your account also helps you to rectify any issues that may crop up throughout the cruise.

Other

59. Pets are not allowed on most cruise ships.
60. Check where you can smoke aboard, and this includes e-cigarettes.
61. Do not invite unauthorised crew into your cabin, or go into crew areas unless authorised.
62. On disembarkation day you will be required to leave your cabin in the morning and wait in the departure lounge until you are called. The places and times for these will be made evident to you whilst aboard. Make sure everything is paid and you have checked your cabin and safe for any valuables.
63. Give yourself enough time to have something to

eat before disembarking, because it can be a long day, especially if you are taking a flight.

33

Positions Aboard

I would like to say at the outset of this chapter, that this is not a definitive list of the positions on a cruise ship and there are certainly many more. I probably haven't placed all crewmember positions in their correct order of authority either, but I have done my best. If someone should take offence at being missed out completely on the list, or they have been placed below another position, I offer my apologies.

Hopefully this chapter will give you some idea of the extent of positions there are on many cruise ships today. I would like to take this opportunity to thank some learned friends who provided me with plenty of information on this subject – you know who you are!

The Captain/Master

The captain - is the highest ranking officer on the ship and he/she has the full authority to make decisions in order to preserve the life and safety of the ship's company and passengers.

Deck Department

The Staff Captain - is the second in command aboard the cruise ship and Head of the Deck Department.

The Safety Officer - is responsible for passenger and crew safety drills, abandon ship procedures, crew safety training, supervision of ships tenders, instructions on safety of all shipboard personnel, with particular reference to emergency procedures.

The Environmental Conservation Officer (ECO) - is a three-stripe, non-watch standing officer responsible for oversight and verification of the cruise line environmental policies, the training, implementation, and verification of regulatory compliance as it relates to applicable environmental laws.

The Officer of the Watch (OOW)- is a designated navigation officer and on behalf of the Master is responsible for all navigational and watch keeping issues.

The 2nd Officer - is a two-stripe Navigation and Watch Keeping Officer and Bridge Team Member.

The 3rd Officer - is an assistant to the OOW or the Junior Watch Keeping Officer on the ship. Reports to the Officer of the Watch (either 1st or 2nd Officer) for navigation and watch keeping aspects and to the Staff Captain.

Apprentice Deck Officer - The candidates for Apprentice Deck Officer must be Nautical School students or graduates who are seeking practical experience or young Navigation Officers working aboard ships.

The Chief Security Officer - is a three-stripe officer who is in charge of implementing the company security policies and all security operations on board the cruise ship both at sea and while in port. He/she must be professionally trained security expert, familiar with illegal drugs trafficking, and anti-terrorist countermeasures.

The Deputy Security Officer - is a two-stripe officer. His/her main responsibility is to control and supervise all points of entry to the cruise ship - gangways and tender docking stations.

The Security Guard - controls points of entry to the ship and the screening process of guests, crew and their luggage. While the ship is in port the Security Guard operates at the Gangway, while on anchor.

The Boson - or also named Boatswain is an experienced sailor and the head of the unlicensed deck crew (ratings) aboard the cruise ship.

The Quartermaster - also named Helmsman is an unlicensed member of the deck crew, an Able Seaman who is performing also Bridge Watch Keeping duties.

The Able Seaman - is a non-officer member of the deck crew (deck rating position) responsible for routine maintenance of the deck and hull of the ship, operation of tenders, lifeboats and rescue boats.

The Ordinary Seaman - is is an unlicensed member of the deck department of the cruise ship.

Engineering Department

The Engineers - are also called technical officers. They are responsible for keeping the ship and the machinery running.

Chief Engineer - is the official title of someone qualified to oversee the engine department. He/she is responsible for all operations and maintenance that have to do with all machinery and equipment throughout the ship. He/she may be paid on par with the captain, although they are never responsible for the action of ship.

The 2nd Engineer or first assistant engineer is the officer responsible for supervising the daily maintenance and operation of the engine department.

The 2nd Assistant - is usually in charge of boilers, fuel, auxiliary engines, condensate and feed systems, and is the third most senior marine engineer on board.

The – 4th Engineer the most junior marine engineer of the ship, he/she is usually responsible for electrical, sewage treatment, lube oil, bilge, and oily water separation systems.

The Motorman - is an unlicensed member of the engine department, with more experience than an Oiler.

The Oiler - is an unlicensed member of the engine department, with more experience than a Wiper.

The Wiper - is an unlicensed member of the engine department, usually with the least experience.

Electro-Technical Department

The Electro-technical officer sometimes referred to as the electrical engineer or simply electrician is in charge of all the electrical systems on the ship.

Steward's Department

The Chief steward directs, instructs, and assigns personnel performing such functions as preparing and serving meals; cleaning and maintaining officers' quarters and steward department areas; and receiving, issuing, and inventorying stores. The chief steward may also plan menus, compiles supply, overtime, and cost control records.

The Chief cook - is generally a senior unlicensed crew member working in the steward's department of a ship.

Medical Department

Chief Doctor – responsible for all medial decisions onboard and reports directly to the captain.

Assistant Doctor – responsible for medical decisions and answers to chief medical doctor.

Nurse/Nurses – there may be a few present on a cruise ship and they answer to the chief doctor.

Passenger Related Positions

Cruise Director, Shore Excursion Managers, Disc Jockeys, Expedition Leaders, Hosts and Hostesses, Naturalists, Water Sports Instructors, Youth Counsellors, Cosmetologist, Fitness Directors, Air/Sea Reservation Agents, Bartenders, Gift Shop Positions, Photographers/videographers, Junior Assistant Pursers, Information Technology Staff, Administration Assistants, Customer Service Representatives, Casino Staff, Cruise

Staff, Entertainers, Gentleman Host, Lecturers, Production Managers, Shore Excursion Staff, Lifeguards, Beauticians, Massage Therapists, Fitness Instructors, Personal Trainers, Bar Stewards, Bedroom Stewards, Hospitality or Hotel Managers, Deckhands, Pursers, Dance Instructors, Booking Agents, Sales and Marketing Positions, art auctioneer, and assistant positions.

Food and Beverage Department

Baker, Bar Back, Bar Manager, Bar Tender, Buffet Server, Butcher, Busboys, Chef de Parie, Cocktail Server, Dining Room Head Waiter, Dining Room Manager, Executive Chef, Food and Beverages Manager, Maitre d' Hotel, Pastry Chef, Sous Chef, Wine Steward.

Housekeeping Department

Cabin Steward, Chief Cabin Steward, Chief Steward Housekeeping, Laundry Staff.

Hotel Administration Department

Accountant, Bellman, IT Manager, Gift Shop Manager, Gift shop Sales Assistant, Hotel Manager, Programme Coordinator, Receptionist.

Personal Care Department

Beauty Therapist, Hair Stylist, Manicurist, Massage Therapist, Spa Attendant.

34

Nautical Terms

This chapter has been included in this book because I was often amazed by how little some passengers knew about the ship they were on. Did you notice I used 'ship' and not 'boat' as to fail to use the right noun whilst onboard might see you being thrown overboard by the Captain. By including the nautical terms, together with their description, you might be able to come to the aid of the ship if you suddenly hear a call over the sound system asking, 'can anyone help steer this ship as the captain and the other officers on the bridge have become incapacitated and can no longer sail it. Is there anyone onboard who knows what to do?'

You can immediately put your hand up and say, 'I do! Just let me run into my cabin and grab my Survival Guide to Cruising, and I will be with you in a jiffy.'

I say this because if I were writing a guidebook called Survival Guide to Taking a Commercial Flight, you would be just as qualified to take the captains seat, and land any jet or plane into the busiest airport, and still feel confident enough to flirt with the cabin staff.

Nautical Terms

Abaft - Towards the stern. **Aboard** - The inside of a ship.

About - the situation of a ship as soon as she has tacked or turned around. **Abreast -** two or more ships lying with their sides parallel. **Adrift** - the state of a ship is not under steam and not attached to moorings. **Aft** - behind, or near the stern of the ship. **After** - a phrase applied to any object in the hinder part of the ship. **A ground -** when a ships bottom, or any part of it, rests in the ground. **A head** - any thing which is situated on that point of the compass to which a ship's stern is said to be a-head of her. **Along side -** side by side of another ship. **A midships** - the middle of a ship. **At anchor** - ship riding at her anchor. **Astern** - any distance behind a ship. **Athwart** - across the line of a ship's course or keel. **Avast** - The command to stop, or cease, in any operation. **Ballast** – the weight at the bottom of a ship to counter the top. **Bearing -** the situation of one place from another, with regard to the points of the compass. **Bear a-hand** - make haste, dispatch. **To bear in with the land** - ship sails towards the shore. **To bear off** - to thrust or keep off the ship's side. **To bear up or away** - changing a ship's course. **Forward** -towards the fore part of a ship. **To founder -** to sink at sea by filling with water. **To freshen** - when a gale increases it is said to freshen. **Gangway** - the entering place into a ship. **Garboard streak** - the streak nearest to the keel. **Grappling-iron** - a thing in the nature of an anchor, with four or six flukes to it. **Grave the ship** - To take off barnacles and other growth from ships bottom/hull. **Grounding** - running a-ground accidentally or not. **Ground-tackle** - every thing belonging to a ship's anchors. **Ground-tier** - that is, the tier which is lowest in the hold. **Gunnel** - the large plank that runs along upon the upper part of a ship's side. **Guy** -

a rope fixed to keep any thing in its place. **Harbor** - a secure place for a ship to anchor. **Hard a-lee** - the situation of the helm, which pushed close to the lee side of the ship. **To haul** - to pull a rope. **To haul the wind** - to direct the ship's course nearer to the point from which the wind blows. **Hawse** - the situation of the cables before the ship's stem, when she is moored with two anchors out from forwards. **Hawser** - a small kind of cable. **Head-fast** - a rope employed to confine the head of a ship to a wharf or some other ship. **Helm** - the instrument by which the ship is steered, and includes both the wheel and the tiller, as one general term. **High-and-dry** - the situation of a ship when so far run a-ground as to be seen dry upon the strand. **Hitch** - to make fast. **Hold** - is the space between the lower deck and the bottom of a ship and where her stores are. **Hull** - the body of the ship. **Jack** - the union flag. **Kedge** - a small anchor. **Keel** - the principal piece of timber on which the vessel is built. **Keel-haul** - to drag a person backwards and forwards under a ship's keel, for certain offences (such as hitting irritating passengers with lobsters). **To keep away** - to alter the ship's course to one rather more large. **Knippers** - a large kind of platted rope. **Knot** - A division of the knot-line, answering, in the calculation of the ship's velocity, to one mile. Overhand knot, wall-knot, diamond knot. **Laden in bulk** - freighted with a cargo. **Laid up** - the situation of a ship when moored in a harbour. **Large** - the wind is on the quarter or abaft the beam. With the wind free when studding sail will draw. **Launch-ho** - to let go the top rope. **Lanyards of the shrouds** - are the small ropes at the ends of them, by which they are hove taut, or tight. **Larboard** -the left side of a ship, looking towards the head. **Larboard-tack** - the situation of a ship when sailing with the wind blowing upon her larboard side. **Lash** - to bind. **Lead line** - a rope with a lead weight attached to measure the depth of water. **Leading-wind** - a fair wind for a ship's course. **Lee** - that part of the hemisphere to which the wind is directed. **Lee-lurches** - the sudden and violent rolls which a ship often takes to leeward in a high sea; particularly when a large wave strikes her on the weather-side. **To leeward** - towards that part of the horizon to which the wind blows. **To lie along** - to be pressed down sideways by a weight of sail in a fresh wind. **List** - the ship moves to one side. **Lizard** - a bight of a small line pointed on a large one. **Log, and Log-line** - by which the ship's path is measured, and her rate of going ascertained. **Monkey** - a small wooden cask to hold rum. **Mooring** - securing a ship in a particular station by chains or cables, which are either fastened to an adjacent shore, or to anchors at the bottom. **Muster** - to assemble. **Neap-tides** - the lowest tides when the moon is at the first or third quarters. **Over-board** - out of the ship; as, he fell overboard, meaning he fell out of, or from, the ship. **Painter** - a rope attached to the bows of a boat, used to make her fast. **Pitching** - the movement of a ship, by which she plunges her head and after-part alternately into the hollow of the sea. **Poop** - the deck next above the quarter-deck. **Port** - used for larboard, or the left side; also a harbour or haven. **Port** - a name given on some occasions to the larboard side of the ship. **Preventer -** an extra rope, to assist another. **Purchase** - any sort of mechanical power employed in raising or removing heavy bodies. **Purchase** - to purchase the anchor, is to loosen it out of the ground. **Quarters** - the several stations of a ship's crew in time of action. **Quartering** - when a ship under sail has the wind blowing on her quarter. **To raise** - to elevate any distant object at sea by approaching it. **Ratlines** - the small ropes fastened to the shrouds, by which the men go aloft. **Reach** - the distance between any two points on the banks of a river. **Ready about -** all the hands are to be attentive, and at their stations for tacking. **Rolling** - the motion by which a ship rocks from side to side like a cradle. **Shank-painter** - the rope by which the shank of the anchor is held up to the ship's side. **To shape a course** - to direct or appoint the track of a ship, in order to prosecute a voyage. **To ship** - to take any person, goods, or thing, on board. **Ship shape** - doing anything in a sailor-like manner. **Shoal** - shallow, not deep. **Sound** - to try the depth of water. **Splice** - to make two ends of ropes fast together by untwisting them, and then putting the strands of one piece with the strands of the other. **Squall** - a sudden violent blast of wind. **To stand on** - to continue advancing. **To stand in** - to advance towards the shore. **To stand off** - to recede from the shore. **Starboard** - the right-hand side of the ship, when looking forward. **To tack** - to turn a ship about from one tack to another, by bringing her head to the wind. **Tiller** - a large piece of wood, or beam, put into the head of the rudder, and by means of which the rudder is moved. **Transom** - a large piece of timber fastened to the stern-posts, to the ends of which the afterpart of the bends are fastened. **Traverse** - to go backwards and forwards. **Veer** – the wind veers, that is, it shifts or changes. **To weigh anchor** - to heave up an anchor from the bottom. **Weigh** - to haul up; as, weigh the anchor. **Yawing** - the motion of a ship when she deviates from to the right or left. **Yards** - the timbers upon which the sails are spread. **Yarn** – rope spliced.

These certainly aren't the full compliment of nautical terms, but at least they give you an idea of what someone is talking about if you suddenly hear them shout, 'will you throw me the ratline, with nippers whilst the ship is laid up, and lash it to the poop so the ship doesn't list over leeward, causing it to bear off and go ballast up?'

35

Questions Not to Ask a Captain

This is a list of questions that I just couldn't resist inserting into this guidebook. It is certainly a bit silly, and not in good taste, however, all of these questions have been asked of captains and officers at some point in their career (although I have used a little licence for comic effect occasionally).

If you are, or have been a captain or an officer, and you feel it is malicious slander – I would suggest you stop taking yourself too seriously!

1. I thought you were a man? – This was said to a woman officer.
2. How long have you worked on this little boat (not ship) for?
3. Is that a toupee you are wearing, make sure you hold on to it as the wind is strong?
4. You don't look like a captain – are you really one?
5. Are you having an affair onboard?
6. Did you get your beautiful partner because of your position?
7. Are you tall enough to be a captain?
8. Have you heard what your crew are saying about you?
9. Have you ever crashed a ship?
10. Have you ever thought of sorting out your bad breath?

11. That uniform makes you look rather obese, have you put on weight lately?
12. How much do you earn?
13. What was your last bonus?
14. Does your partner know about your other woman/man?
15. Could you let me drive the boat out of harbour tomorrow, because let's face it, your pretty bad at it yourself?
16. Can I swap cabins with you on this cruise because mine is tiny?
17. Do you always say something to the passengers because I wouldn't bother in future, you are such an awful speaker?
18. I suppose you thought you were being funny didn't you?
19. How did you get your captains certificate because I was told by your first officer that it probably came from the back of a cornflake box?
20. Can you tie my shoe lace for me please, I just don't feel like bending over?
21. Can I pull at your hair to see if it is real?
22. Shouldn't you be retired by now?
23. Do they let people as old as you in charge of a big ship like this normally?
24. You aren't called Captain Crash are you?
25. Do you mind if I make fun of you to impress my girlfriend/boyfriend?
26. What is it like knowing you are getting fired in a couple of days?
27. Can I give you some advice…don't give up your

day job.

28. Does your mum know you are such a dictator onboard with your crew, I am sure she would have something to say about it if she did?
29. Is this your first ship, I can give you some lessons on driving a boat if it would help, because I have rowed a blow up dinghy?

If you do decide to use some of these suggestions with captains, I would like you to do me a favour.

Keep my name out of it please?

36

Tick List (Things to Take)

You might like to use this handy tick list before setting off on your cruise. Obviously there is no need to take everything that is mentioned. I have also left some space at the end for you to add some of your own items should you wish.

- o **Lightweight cases** – or holdall/sports bag with wheels.
- o **Passport** - with at least 6 months on it.
- o **Visa** - for any countries you may be visiting.
- o **Printed paperwork** - which may be relevant for either confirmation of activities, or specific add-ons you have included on the cruise.
- o **Photocopy** – of passport and driving licence if they are required on the cruise.
- o **Formal clothes** – depending upon cruise, and children may need them too.
- o **Clothes** – remembering to pack for any eventuality, and for the air-conditioning as it can be a little cold at times.
- o **Jacket** – waterproof.
- o **Casual clothes** – for none lido deck activities.
- o **Shoes** – all purpose/formal.
- o **Belt** – standard or special money belt.
- o **Sandals** – or suitable flat shoes.
- o **Swimming costumes** – at least 2 per person,

because they can take a while to dry in your cabin.

- **Travel Insurance** – for each individual.
- **Mobile Phone** – with splash cover if not waterproof.
- **Tablet** – or laptop including a splash cover.
- **Bank Cards** – preferably 2 separate ones.
- **Cash** – in correct currency for cruise.
- **Sun cream** – if you are allergic bring extra as you might not be able to purchase it whilst away.
- **Hat** – they can get blown off on ship, so make sure it is tight on your head, or held on in some way.
- **Gloves** – in cold climates
- **Medication** – have some packed in your carry-on bag for the times when you don't have access to your cases.
- **Small bills** – dollars or similar for tips.
- **Power strip** – to attach all your chargers and appliances in your cabin, as sockets can be minimal on some cruise ships.
- **Power Adapter** – relevant to the cruise you are going on (European/US for instance).
- **Torch** – or use mobile phone.
- **Ear plugs** – if you want to sleep during the day.
- **Seasickness medication** – wrist-band, patches, pills and other things that might work for you.
- **Coffee mug** – none breakable and insulated.
- **Cloth bags** – for purchases etc.
- **Rucksack** – cloth/leather ones take up less space.
- **Warm clothing** – at least one.
- **Small umbrella** – because it can rain in any place.
- **Camera** – including extra batteries and charger.

- **Tags** – on bags with contact details.
- **Drivers Licence** – make sure it can be used in the country you are going to if you are going to rent transport.
- **Coat hangers** – wire or cardboard take up very little space in your luggage bag.
- **Magnets** – hooked and flat.
- **First aid kit** – small one with some essential items.
- **Laundry alternatives** – if you have allergies.
- **Stationary** – pens, highlighter, small notebook, pencils.
- **Children's documents** – passports and other essential documents for them.
- **Fix it stuff** – duct tape and such like, as things break or come apart.
- **Strap** – to go around case as zips can break.
- **Insect repellent** – bites and stings happen anywhere.
- **Walky-talky** – to contact each other aboard rather than using a mobile phone.
- **Sunglasses** – UV properties for cold and warm climates.
- **Watch/timepiece** – more than one.
- **Chargers** – for devices such as tablet/mobiles/razors etc.
- **Neck wallet** – for passports/money/small documents.
- **Lanyard** – for cabin cards.
- **Lip balm** – air conditioning can dry out lips.
- **Books** – physical or download ones.
- **Washing bag** – including toiletries.

Things to be Mindful Of

- **Cruise contact details** – and mobile numbers, leave with family/friends.
- **Read information provided by cruise company/agent** - thoroughly when you receive it, including your contract.
- **All Inclusive** – see what is included in an all inclusive offer.
- **Places and ports** – start reading about them so you know what to expect when you arrive.
- **Contact mobile provider** – prior to your cruise to organise how best to make any calls and service charges more affordable.
- **Phone settings** – know how to adjust them for the cruise to reduce unnecessary costs.
- **Carry on bag and contents** – wash bag, change of clothes, swimwear, sunglasses, money including small notes, flat shoes, sun cream, and anything else you feel you might need when you don't have access to your main luggage.
- **Bag for sealing liquids** – place all liquids in special sealing reusable bag. Remembering not to take it as hand luggage if flying.
- **Space saving when packing** – utilise shoes for bottles and small items, roll your clothes, (they don't crease as easy) be neat with your packing, and leave space for things to bring home.
- **Take a photograph** – of luggage so you can show what it looks like if it gets lost.

- **Lightweight case or bag** – can mean you have more available weight to carry more items with you.
- **Take valuables** - out of safe at the end of the cruise.
-
-
-
-
-
-
-
-
-
-
-
-
-
-
-
-
-
-
-
-
-

Acknowledgments

I would like to take this opportunity to thank everyone that has given of their time and expertise in assisting me with this book.

Printed in Great Britain
by Amazon

33703727R00128